Underdogs
and
Outsiders

Underdogs
and
Outsiders

A Bible Study on the Untold Stories of Advent

TOM FUERST

Abingdon Press / Nashville

Underdogs and Outsiders
A Bible Story on the Untold Stories of Advent
By Tom Fuerst
Copyright © 2016 by Abingdon Press
All rights reserved.

ISBN-13: 9781501824289

16 17 18 19 20 21 22 23 24 25—10 9 8 7 6 5 4 3 2 1

Manufactured in the United States of America

For my mom,
in hope of the promise
that all your suffering and grief
can be swept up into God's good purposes in Christ.

CONTENTS

INTRODUCTION

Advent reminds us year after year that the Savior of the world did not come into perfect families, filled with perfect people, who did not need saving to begin with. He came into families like yours and mine, families with immediate wounds and generational scars, families with a pedigree only God could love. In other words, Advent reminds us that the Savior of the world loves being right in the mix of human activity, finding redemptive possibilities in all our missteps, misspeaks, and mistakes. If your family is anything like mine, you know it takes a heart such as God's to patiently work with and redeem some of the things we would all rather keep hidden.

We encounter this reality right at the beginning of the New Testament, where the Book of Matthew opens with a genealogy of Jesus. The Messiah's family tree, we will find, is full of underdogs and outsiders, a number of unexpected people through whom God has worked in powerful ways. By mentioning these people in Jesus' family, Matthew communicates something powerful to us about who Jesus is.

When I entered eighth grade, my family lived for a stint in some low-income apartments in Bloomington, Indiana. The apartment building was framed as a square with a courtyard in the middle, and the apartment doors faced inward toward the courtyard, allowing residents to live walled off from the rest of society. This isolation created our own little ecosystem of drama.

My family largely avoided the drama, which often culminated in fist fights. I do not intend to communicate by this that we lacked theatrical impulse, but merely that we were a family of lovers, not fighters. Still, mom and I played our part in the melodrama one day. My mother and our neighbor engaged in a shouting match because of some owed money. Degrading language dominated their name-calling contest, which climaxed in the man wielding the rhetorical trump card: *"I bet none of your four children even have the same father!"*

I passively stood by until that moment. As an eighth grader whose only knowledge of fighting came from Sting and the Macho Man Randy Savage, I had no chance against a thirty-five year old man. But once he sounded those words—once he insulted my mother's integrity—I crouched into my best WWE fighting position, stepped in front of my mother, and gave him my best comeback: "We do too have the same dad! *You* don't even have the same dad!"

Look, you can read that sentence a thousand more times and it still will not make sense. It does not make sense now. It did not make sense at the time. It never will. But I felt so fired up that it did not matter if I made sense. I championed my mom's character, and my own. You see, an unspoken cultural universal reveals itself in this story: No matter the argument, one can always escalate the situation by insulting an opponent's parent or family of origin. If you insult my heritage, if you question my family tree, then you cut me in one of the gravest ways possible. In doing so, you call into question my worth as a person.

In light of this universal norm, the family tree of Jesus in Matthew Chapter 1 should shock us. What could stand in sharper contrast to the coming Savior of the world than a family tree packed with people who fall woefully short of our notions of "traditional family values" and live outside our racial and religious boundaries? Matthew seems to introduce the Christmas story by insulting Jesus' family!

We moderns find genealogical records a bore, but ancient persons placed a high value on them because they did not have photo albums. These names and the stories associated with them gave ancients a place in the world. Grandparents pulled grandkids onto their laps and walked through the family tree. With each name the child's eyes brightened; with each story the child's heritage came alive. Each line led to the next until that child knew his or her place in the world. But genealogies did not just tell a child who belonged in the family; they also told the child who did not. Genealogies were selective: Certain behavior could get you left out. In this way, the genealogy served as a moral warning to the child: Don't mess around like Uncle Bill, he got ousted from the family tree. In a sense, genealogies acted less like a formal government document and more like the photos hanging in our hallways. We do not put everyone in our family on display in the hall. We do not want to stare at crazy Uncle Bill every time we go through the corridor, and we certainly do not want company asking questions about him. So we filter our photos just as ancient people filtered genealogies. If great grandpa fought next to King David against the Philistines, his name undoubtedly found its way onto the list. But if great grandpa shamed the family with illicit acts of Ba'al worship, then his family blotted his name from the family tree. Genealogies do not report naked facts. They collect specific facts to tell a specific story.

We can ask, then, what story Matthew wishes to tell through the genealogy of Jesus that he presents. It's a story we might not expect, because it's a genealogy full of underdogs and outsiders. By providing Jesus' pedigree, Matthew places Jesus within the ambiguous world of sinners and saints—providing us with the fodder we need to rhetorically trump card him in a courtyard shouting match. And therein lies the intrigue of Jesus' lineage. In his family we find cheaters, liars, idolaters, heroes, villains, broken people, messy stories, and (gasp!) Gentiles.

Abraham fathered our faith, but in his impatience he tried to bring about the promises of God by sleeping with a slave woman. Jacob swindled his brother out of his inheritance and stole their father's blessing for himself. King David slept with another man's wife, then murdered him.

By including these suspect personalities in Jesus' family tree, Matthew captures something important about the nature of Advent. Advent reminds us that God enters into the awkward, ambiguous, sketchy parts of human existence, redeeming humankind from the inside out. Jesus Christ did not come into a perfect family filled with perfect people who didn't need saving. He came into a wrecked family filled with wrecked people who needed a Savior. By displaying the broken branches on Christ's family tree, God sheds light on the realities of the human condition.

This Advent study focuses on just a few of the broken branches: the unlikely heroines of the story. We don't often hear these stories during Advent. But the stories of the five women in Christ's lineage—Tamar, Rahab, Ruth, Bathsheba, and Mary—embody the reality into which Christ came and the Advent hope we can find within it. Had Matthew wanted a cleaner, more clearly Jewish sampling, he could have worked with Sarah, Rebekah, Leah, or Rachel.[1] But Matthew wants to show this Savior came for everyone, including underdogs and outsiders.

Through the wombs of four Gentile women and a teenage, Jewish girl, God gave Advent hope to the world. This hope proclaims that our pasts, including our families of origin, can be taken up and become a part of our future in Christ.

---

1. From *The Gospel of Matthew*, by Craig Keener (Eerdmans, 2009); page 78.

CHAPTER 1

Tamar
Girl Interrupting

Key Scripture: Genesis 38

As I entered third grade, my family moved to a small town in the middle of Missouri. Every once in a while, my mom put my siblings and me on the bus to attend a local Lutheran church. Mom cared very little about us catching religion; she just enjoyed the free childcare for two hours a week. As a single mom, she found that time alone proved to be a precious commodity. Unfortunately for her, this free childcare only lasted a few months, because one day the children's minister sent a letter home to my mom. The letter said that her children had behavioral issues, and if our mom had no intention of attending with us then she could not send us back.

Shaming a single mother into attending church seems like an odd church growth tactic. Besides, don't churches with bus ministries expect the children they pick up to have some behavioral issues? At any rate, I had no problem with not going back. Even as early as third grade, I felt out of place at church. My family had no "good" Christian people. The realities of divorce, poverty, and dysfunction screamed from my soul on Sunday mornings.

In the seventeen years I have walked with Christ, I have learned an important truth that stands in sharp contrast with what I learned from that church in my childhood: Jesus Christ did not come into a perfect family filled with perfect people who did not need saving. He came into a messed up family filled with messed up people who needed a Savior just like me. He came to invite the very people whose behavioral issues would have incurred a dis-invitation letter from a church where everyone behaves properly. That reality stands at the center of our Advent hope that God is and always will be with us. And it's a reality to which Matthew points his readers by including misfits in the genealogy of Jesus.

We readily remember that Jesus ate with people who had behavioral issues, like tax collectors and prostitutes. Yet somehow we often overlook that one of his great grandmothers took such behavioral issues to an all-new level. Tamar, the first woman and Gentile mentioned in Jesus' family tree, somehow made prostitution *righteous*.

An Unexpected Interlude

Unpacking grandma Tamar's story begins with understanding the larger narrative in which we first encounter her in Genesis 38. Tamar's story stands as an interruption in the story of Joseph and his brothers, found in Genesis 37–50. The writer of Genesis has just told us of Joseph's brothers selling him into Egypt as a slave in Chapter 37, and we sense that we are in for a long story. Then, suddenly, the author of Genesis shifts gears and interrupts the Joseph narrative with one of the strangest stories in all of Scripture. Before we read about Joseph's ups and downs in Egypt (Genesis 39–41), we encounter a story about one of Joseph's brothers. In Genesis 38, the author turns from Joseph to Judah, who has already shown his character flaws. It was Judah who suggested selling

Joseph into slavery so that he and his brothers could turn a profit and be rid of their despised younger brother (Genesis 37:26-28). Judah is the kind of guy who would spearhead the plan to sell his brother into slavery, then watch his father grieve for a son who had not really died (Genesis 37:31-35).

When Genesis 38 opens, we read that Judah "moved away from his brothers" (38:1). The story goes on to tell us that Judah married a Canaanite woman (38:2), something that his father and grandfather both avoided (Genesis 24:3, 28:1). Jacob and Isaac both married members of their extended family in Haran, which their fathers desired. Judah, however, followed in the steps of his uncles, Ishmael and Esau, both of whom married Canaanite women and both of whom eventually became separated from God's chosen people. This spells nothing but trouble for Judah. By moving away from his family and pursuing, in this marriage, the ways of his uncles, Judah has separated himself both symbolically and physically from Abraham's lineage, the lineage of God's promise (see Genesis 12:1-3).

Judah's marriage to a Canaanite woman results in three sons: Er, Onan, and Shelah. Judah's oldest son Er marries a woman named Tamar. Though Genesis does not explicitly tell us that she is a Canaanite, it can be inferred because Judah is living among the Canaanites and away from his brothers. Ancient readers of Genesis would have considered Tamar, as a Canaanite, to be morally suspect. But it is Er's wickedness, not Tamar's, that draws attention from God: "But the LORD considered Judah's oldest son Er immoral, and the LORD put him to death" (Genesis 38:7). The nature of Er's evil remains a mystery. All we can know is that he must have enacted some entirely egregious evil. After all, he is the first individual God kills directly in the entire Bible.

The Wronged Woman

The death of Er creates an enormous problem for Tamar. In the patriarchal culture of the ancient Near East, a woman found her identity and security in the men in her life. First her father, then her husband, and finally her sons protected her, provided for her, and gave her a future. To put it in modern terms: They provided the income, the insurance, and the retirement plan. Women had few other options. This, of course, made the status of widows and women who couldn't bear children tenuous. When Er dies, he and Tamar have not produced a male child together. This leaves Tamar without a husband or son. She is in the vulnerable social position of a childless widow. Her husband had been Judah's oldest son, and he would have inherited the lion's share of Judah's estate. Tamar would have been fairly well-off. But after the death of Er, her future prospects are suddenly gone. Without a husband or a son, her status as an insider to Judah's clan comes into question.

Fortunately, in an effort to protect widows from a life of perpetual poverty, there was a custom that provided security for women in a situation like Tamar's. We see this custom reflected here in Genesis 38 and in the Book of Ruth. It eventually became a part of Israelite law. Deuteronomy 25:5-10 explains this law, called the "Levirate Law." According to this law, if a man died without having a son,

> the dead man's wife must not go outside the family and marry a stranger. Instead, her brother-in-law should go to her and take her as his wife. He will then consummate the marriage according to the brother-in-law's duty. The brother-in-law will name the oldest male son that she bears after his dead brother so that his brother's legacy will not be forgotten in Israel. (Deuteronomy 25:5-6)

In this way, the deceased brother's lineage continued, his property was passed down, and his widow found security and a future. In other words, the Levirate Law maintained and protected the fabric of society by preserving the family and providing for those who found themselves economically and socially vulnerable. This custom acted as an ancient form of life insurance before such a thing existed. We may not find this an ideal situation, especially in our culture that values freedom of choice, particularly in regard to the person we marry. Nevertheless, in an ancient setting where widows had few options to support themselves, this was an attempt to create a more just society.

So, in accordance with the custom that preluded the Levirate Law, Judah does the right thing by giving his next oldest son to Tamar in marriage. He tells his son, Onan, "Go to your brother's wife, do your duty as her brother-in-law, and provide children for your brother" (Genesis 38:8). Notice, "Judah does not say to Onan, 'marry her,' just, 'go in to her,' or, 'have sex with her.' The father appeals to Onan's sense of sympathy by referring to the late Er as *your brother* rather than as 'my son.' Judah's concern plainly lies with his dead son, not with his living daughter-in-law."[1] In Judah's language we hear no compassion for Tamar. He regards her as mere property, another thing to deal with—an inconvenience. He may as well tell Onan his deceased brother left him a collection of knickknacks in the attic.

Not surprisingly, then, Onan treats Tamar in exactly the same manner. This obligation to provide children for her and his deceased brother provides a greater headache for him than for his father. By taking on this responsibility, Onan puts his (and his sons') own inheritance at risk. As the oldest son, Er had the right to a double portion of his father's estate upon Judah's death. That larger share would have passed to Onan after Er's death, but the Levirate Law now called that into question. Presumably, the children Onan provided for Er would receive Er's inheritance. To do the right thing, Onan must forfeit his potential personal gain. Tamar represents a financial liability, a threat to his inheritance. So, calculating the cost of impregnating Tamar, Onan has sex with her, but at the last second, "he wasted his semen on the ground, so he wouldn't give his brother children" (Genesis 38:9).

Social complexities abound in this decision. Onan's motivations have nothing to do with responsible family planning. By refusing to impregnate Tamar, puts his own interests above those of Tamar and the rest of his family. Onan makes an active choice to deny Tamar justice and leave her in a position of vulnerability, where her safety, identity, and future remain questionable. He does this all because he wants more for himself and his own children. But the worst part of Onan's actions might even remain unstated by the writer of Genesis. The Levirate Law provided a way out for men who did not want to take responsibility for their deceased brother's wife (Deuteronomy 25:7-10). It involved some community shaming, where the brother-in-law would be publicly identified as someone who refused to build up his brother's family. But denying justice to the vulnerable ought to cause shame. Onan, however, circumvents the repercussions of his refusal by spilling his semen on the ground. In short, Onan appears to live justly while actually denying justice to Tamar, which adds to his decadence and her destitution. His injustice appears as justice, his darkness charades as light, and his malevolence masks itself as benevolence. But God sees through his deception, and "The LORD considered what he did as wrong and put him to death too" (Genesis 38:10).

As if things could not get any worse for Tamar, Judah's lack of empathy hits overdrive with the death of his second son. This woman, in his thinking, has brought a curse upon his household. He does not assume his two sons must have done something wicked; he assumes instead that Tamar is to blame. This exacerbates the injustice of Tamar's situation because Judah, then, refuses to send his third son, Shelah, to sleep with her. "He thought Shelah would die like his brothers had" (Genesis 38:11). Judah thus ensures Tamar's perpetual vulnerability. The social structures meant to ease her situation had instead solidified her sufferings, because first Onan and then Judah put their interests ahead of hers. Rather than protecting the victim, Judah blames the victim. Instead of acknowledging his sons' evil, Judah faults Tamar for their demise. So he sends her back home to live with her father, deflecting his responsibility for her welfare. Judah then tells her he intends to send for her when his youngest son comes of age. Of course, he has no such intention. And Tamar knows this. She knows that by withholding an opportunity for her to give birth, Judah has left her with no status and no future.

Taking Matters Into Her Own Hands

What should Tamar have done? How could a woman like this survive in a world where men held all the cards? Should she just fold, turn in her cards, and give up? If that's what she should have done, Tamar did not get the memo. Instead, she got creative. As Helen Pearson says, "Perhaps tired of having men make decisions for her—tired of being given away and then given back, tired of being told what to do and where to go—Tamar finally refused to be the victim."[2] Tamar took matters into her own hands by arranging to sleep with Judah himself.

Despite her own vulnerability, Tamar created a way to take advantage of Judah at the moment of his greatest vulnerability. Sometime after Judah sent Tamar back to her father's house, Judah's wife died. As a widow, Tamar knew something about the emotional turmoil of losing a spouse. Changing from the clothes and disposition of a widow, Tamar "covered herself with a veil" and "put on makeup" (Genesis 38:14). Other ways of translating that last part include "perfumed herself" or "wrapped herself up" (CEB alternate translations). The meaning is clear: She makes herself attractive. She then went and sat at the entrance of Enaim, where Judah would pass by. Her veiled face led Judah to think she was a prostitute (Genesis 38:15). She intended to catch Judah's attention, to provide him a means to address his physical "needs."

Not recognizing the prostitute at the city gate as his Tamar, Judah asks to sleep with her and offers to pay her a goat for her services—a goat which, incidentally, he does not have with him (Genesis 38:16-17). She plays the role of the congenial hostess and proposes he give her his seal, cord, and staff as a guarantee that he would provide the goat. She would have sex with him now, he would leave these items with her, and then later he would bring her the goat and collect his items (Genesis 38:17-18). But these items, Judah's seal, cord, and staff, are hardly insignificant items. They are markers of Judah's identity. As one scholar writes:

"The seal was often threaded onto a leather cord and worn around the neck of the owner. In Palestine it is more common to find stamp seals engraved on the flat side. Another form of identification mentioned here is the staff, an aid to walking as well as an animal goad and weapon. Since this was a personal item, it may well have been carved and polished and thus known to belong to a particular person."[3]

In other words, Judah trades Tamar the equivalent of his social security number and passport. He sleeps with her and leaves these significant items with her. And Tamar becomes pregnant as a result.

Modern Christians might find Tamar's actions offensive, as they fall outside our bourgeois sexual ethic. But to ancient readers, not only would Judah's offense have seemed comparatively more troublesome, but Tamar's actions would have seemed quite, well, righteous. Tamar's actions expose the double standard in ancient (and modern) societies that allow men to use their power irresponsibly and leave the women to deal with the consequences. Victor

Hamilton points out other instances where something similar happens in Scripture. As offensive as it may seem,

> Tamar's taking advantage of Judah for a more noble purpose is not without parallel in the OT. One may think of Esther's exploitation of Ahasuerus's sexual desires for the achievement of her praiseworthy aims, that is, the deliverance of her people. Or one may think of Naomi, the childless widow, playing on Boaz's predictable appreciation of Ruth's beauty. Here then is an instance where the end justifies the means.[4]

From a position of comfort and security, in a world where feminism has done so much to promote women's rights, we may be tempted to judge Tamar's actions severely and by our own cultural values. But as far as the biblical narrative goes, Tamar stands within a long line of women who used the tools they had available to create a better world, preparing the way for a scandalous Messiah. Maybe sometimes the ends do justify the means.

When Judah desires to retrieve his deposit—his seal, cord, and staff—he sends his friend Hirah the Adullamite to pay the woman. Strangely, Hirah does not ask the locals for "the prostitute" but "the consecrated worker" (Genesis 38:20-21). Another translation uses the term "temple prostitute" (NRSV), but the Hebrew word can also mean simply "holy woman." It's unclear exactly why Hirah uses this word instead of "prostitute," which Judah had though Tamar to be (Genesis 38:15). However, it seems likely that he wanted to manage Judah's image: It would look bad to go around publicly inquiring about a prostitute. "Consecrated worker" or "holy woman" sounds much more acceptable. Hirah returns to Judah with the goat because the people of the town don't know the "consecrated worker" of whom he asks. Judah's subsequent actions further illustrate his desire to save face. When Hirah is unable to find the woman Judah has slept with, Judah decides to leave his items with her: "Let her keep everything so we aren't laughed at" (Genesis 38:23). In Bill Arnold's words, Judah is "more concerned about saving face than providing the goat such a woman would have needed for her next meal."[5] His character remains consistent: He shows no concern for justice in the case of his daughter-in-law, and his concern for the economic well-being of this prostitute only extends as far as his reputation, however false, will allow.

"See If You Recognize"

Then, after three months pass, Judah receives some surprising news: Tamar is expecting. A messenger tells Judah, "Your daughter-in-law Tamar has become a prostitute, and is now pregnant because of it." Judah responds by saying, "Bring her out so that she may be burned" (38:24). Judah's harsh response displays the double standard inherent in his culture: Sexual promiscuity among men is not only tolerated but expected. However, in that culture, a women's sexuality remained under the dominion of male authority. In other words, Judah could sleep with a prostitute and receive no punishment. But when his daughter-in-law acted as a prostitute, she deserved to die. Judah's indignation has no basis in righteousness; it merely exists within the cultural bubble of a patriarchal double standard. And this double standard exists precisely because Judah judges Tamar as his property. Property which he now threatens to burn.

Later, Israelite law called for the death penalty for sexual immorality (see Deuteronomy 22:23-24), which seems cruel enough. Yet Judah does not merely seek the death penalty; he seeks a public burning. Judah's judgment on Tamar, then, is jarring, to say the least. He "condemned in Tamar what he excused in himself."[6] His history of unrighteousness a distant thought, his burning rage only cares that she has acted in an unrighteous manner this once. Little does he know that the very terms *righteous* and *unrighteous* are about to get a serious makeover.

When Tamar finds herself at three months pregnant called before her father-in-law, the cunning and creativity of her plan begins to come together in a comedic climax. She sends a messenger ahead of her to prepare for her arrival. The messenger carries with him Judah's personal effects given to Tamar at the time of their encounter, along with a damning message: "I'm pregnant by the man who owns these things. See if you recognize whose seal, cord, and staff these are" (Genesis 38:25). I can imagine the messenger pausing between each item for rhetorical effect: "this seal . . . this cord . . . this staff . . . " Snared now by Tamar's trap, Judah has no other option than to admit these items belong to him. His e-mail address has appeared on the hacked webpage. His profile picture cannot be mistaken for anyone else.

Tamar's words reveal Judah to be a man caught in his own web of wickedness, but they do more than reveal his identity. They assert her identity. They assert her humanity. "Implied in her words is the request that Judah recognize her for who she is: his wronged daughter-in-law."[7] And as surprised as Judah is to see his items coming from the home of Tamar, we, the readers, may be even more surprised at Judah's response. For the first time in the entire narrative, Judah acts in a godly manner: "She's more righteous than I am, because I didn't allow her to marry my son Shelah" (Genesis 38:26).

"She is more righteous than I am." Judah's rhetoric of "righteousness" here seems ironic considering the fact that Tamar acted as a prostitute, but the writer of Genesis wants us to understand that her deviance compares not at all with Judah's denial of justice. As Walter Brueggemann says, "Tamar has committed the kind of sin the 'good people' prefer to condemn—engaging in deception and illicit sex and bringing damage to a good family . . . [But] by his indifference, [Judah] has violated her right to wellbeing and dignity in the community."[8] When we define righteousness and unrighteousness merely in terms of pet sins or religious deeds, we lose the bigger picture of responsibility and obligations toward the weaker members of society. This responsibility and obligation is inherent to the Christian faith. Tamar leaves this story without a single word of condemnation hanging over her reputation. Rather, Judah sees the good of her behavior in a situation where she had few options. Her actions make her righteous, even if they offend our notions of traditional family values and Victorian sexuality.

In fact, even as the writer of Genesis gives Tamar the label "righteous," the larger biblical story shows Tamar in an important role. That is precisely why Tamar appears in Matthew Chapter 1. While the story in Genesis will leave Tamar to follow Joseph and never return back to her, it is not through Joseph's lineage that God saves the world, but Tamar's. One of the twin boys conceived in Tamar's encounter with Judah is named Perez (Genesis 38:27-30). Through Perez eventually comes Boaz; through Boaz comes David; and through David comes Jesus the Messiah (Matthew 1). Through Tamar, then, comes the salvation of the world. Jesus Christ did not come into a perfect family filled with perfect people who did not need saving. He came into a messed up family filled with messed up people who needed a Savior just like you and me.

And therein lies the Advent hope—those of us who know the depths of our imperfections can find grace in a story such as this. Tamar is a Canaanite; she is a childless widow; and she behaves as a prostitute. She is an underdog and outsider if ever there was one. But the ethnic, religious, and moral outsider finds not only acceptance into God's family, but actually becomes part of God's plan to remake the world in true righteousness. This is a righteousness that not only appears religious, but also defines itself in responsibility and obligation to love our neighbors as ourselves, to care for the vulnerable in society. It is a righteousness defined by right relationships and justice.

This often-forgotten text previews the coming Christ by describing an upsidedown world where the defenseless are exalted over the domineering and the marginalized over the mighty. In Christ, prostitutes and sinners find fellowship in a way the "righteous" can never experience. Or rather, maybe they can experience it only insofar as they are willing to acknowledge that those who appear less than righteous may in fact be "more righteous than I am."

Questions for Reflection and Discussion

1. Have you ever encountered a person who seemed immoral or not religious who, after your encounter, you walked away thinking they may be more "righteous" than you? What made this person seem unrighteous? What helped you rethink your original thoughts about them?

2. How does the writer of Genesis seem to evaluate Tamar's sexual activities? What in the biblical story gives you this impression?

3. What transformation do you see in Tamar and in Judah as this story progresses? What hope does that give you?

4. What does it mean for us to hold up Tamar as a model or a heroine? What does Tamar have to teach us about living life in the ambiguous world of Advent?

5. How might this story prepare Matthew's readers to deal with the awkwardness of Mary's pregnancy in the Christmas story?

6. Does it surprise you that Matthew names not only Perez, but his mother Tamar in the genealogy of Jesus? Why do you think this Canaanite woman's name is found in a list dominated by Jewish men?

7. How does the story of this family, so clearly in turmoil, make you feel about what God is doing with your own family? How does this story inspire you to pray for your family and also challenge your family to greater righteousness?

Prayer

Father of our Lord Jesus Christ, we live in a world of injustice and heartache. Death haunts each home and heart, leaving us feeling helpless in its grip. And like Judah, those in our world who should know better often seem apathetic and morally ambiguous. Even your church has found itself many times on the side of the oppressor, straining out moral gnats while swallowing the camels of major sins. And so in the ambiguous world of Advent, we ask you to give us hope. Give us the kind of hope that drove Tamar to act in a way that shocked the "morally responsible" and awed the morally calloused. Drive us to that scandalous manger where a teenage girl gave birth to a baby that was not fathered by her fiancé. And remind us in that baby's ancestry that you did not come into a perfect family filled with perfect people who did not need saving. And therefore you can and will save us through the scandal of Jesus Christ crucified. Amen.

Focus for the Week

This week, reflect on your family. Be honest about any brokenness that lies within it. Be brutally honest. Look around at your interactions with your parents, siblings, children, or other family members, and name those places where God might want to work on some things. As a member of the elect family of God, Judah took his privileges for granted. God still had a lot of work to do in his family, but he stopped paying attention. Make a list of the relationships in your family where you think you are long overdue for some repentance. List names and events that exemplify places of brokenness you'd rather ignore. Then make a plan to pursue righteousness and reconciliation in these relationships, piece by piece, person by person. Some of these may be fixed more quickly than others. Some may never get fixed. Trusting God to work these things out, put yourself in a position to see and follow God's lead. God doesn't work through model families, but through imperfect families like Judah's and Tamar's. It's a messy business, but God is big enough to help us out.

---

1. From *The Book of Genesis Chapters 18-50*, by Victor P. Hamilton (Eerdmans, 1995); page 435.

2. From *Mother Roots*, by Helen Bruch Pearson (Upper Room Books, 2002); page 56.

3. From *The IVP Bible Background Commentary: Old Testament*, by John H. Walton, Victor H. Matthews & Mark W. Chavalas (IVP Academic, 2000); page 70.

4. From *The Book of Genesis Chapters 18-50*, by Victor P. Hamilton (Eerdmans, 1995); page 443.

5. From *Genesis*, by Bill T. Arnold (Cambridge University Press, 2009); page 328.

6. From *Mother Roots*, by Helen Bruch Pearson (Upper Room Books, 2002); page 61.

7. From *Mothers on the Margins?: The Significance of Women in Matthew's Geneaology*, by E. Anne Clements (Pickwick Publications, 2014); page 57.

8. From *Genesis*, by Walter Brueggemann (Westminster John Knox Press, 1982); page 311.

CHAPTER 2

Rahab
God's Working Woman

Key Scripture: Joshua 2

Advent opens our eyes to the ways in which God's love is bigger than we could possibly have imagined. How else can we make sense of God's birth as one of us, joining us in our broken world in order to save it? In the family tree of Jesus we find in Matthew, the name Rahab points to this reality. In her story, we see God's love pushing past the usual boundaries to embrace even Israel's enemies.

When I became a Christian at seventeen years old, God immediately gave me a deep desire to see my family come to know Jesus, too. For years I prayed for my family and shared my faith with them, but none of them seemed interested in the Christian faith. At the time, I had a theological reason to explain why this was the case: God had created my family for the sole purpose of gaining glory through their destruction. This was an answer that one branch of Christian theology—Reformed theology—had reached to the question of why some people never come to know Christ. This theology proposed that God never intended to save my family, to deliver them from evil, or to wrap them in divine love. From the perspective of this theological tradition, God had determined to destroy my dad, mom, sister, and brothers before they were even created. Like the Canaanites in the Book of Joshua, God had set my family on the course to destruction, and whether or not I liked this reality, the only response my theology allowed meant bowing my head and praising God.

I remember the first time I connected these three points: my immersion in Reformed theology, my family's destiny, and the destruction of the Canaanites. I broke down in deep sobs of grief in my kitchen. I could not see how a good God could create my family—or the Canaanites for that matter—for the purpose of destroying them. That fits under no definition of "good" I have ever encountered, especially in the Bible. Such a view of God seemed sadistic and hurtful. That evening in my kitchen not only marked the beginning of my turn away from Reformed theology, but also set me on a quest to understand what God commands the Israelites to do in the Book of Joshua, the Book of Deuteronomy, and other parts of the Bible. It is within one of these troublesome stories that we find the woman Rahab, the second female ancestor of Jesus named in Matthew's genealogy.

No Easy Answers

Quickly, I learned that many Christians before me had wrestled with these passages in the Old Testament, where God orders the Israelites to utterly destroy the Canaanites and other inhabitants of the Promised Land. Some Christians, I found, believed the Israelites misunderstood God, or misunderstood God's command. In other words, God actually never intended the killing of all the Canaanites; Israel simply invented a theology of extermination that allowed them to take the land from its rightful owners. Other Christians surmised that the events within the Book of Joshua did not even happen. They note a lack of historical evidence for a swift, thorough Israelite conquest of the Promised Land. They also point out that the implications about God's character in these passages seem inconsistent with the rest of the Bible. Such readers conclude, therefore, that the stories of Joshua simply do not reflect historical reality.[1] In sum, then, our traditional options for understanding these stories force us to question God's character, Israel's character, or the character of the story Joshua tells. These options are unsettling, to say the least.

It may be more fruitful to lay aside these big-picture questions for a moment, to let the characters within the story have a say. As we will see, the story of Rahab complicates the conquest of Canaan and prevents us from settling for easy answers. After all, the prominence of a righteous Canaanite prostitute at the beginning of this book, juxtaposed as she is with seedy Israelite men, reverses our expectations of who qualifies as "righteous" and who does not. Using that contrast, the author of Joshua raises tough ethical questions and asks us to pause. Joshua offers no blind justification for violence. Instead, Rahab's story provides an opportunity to think closely about all uses of violence or strategies of dehumanization. In a world too cleanly divided between sinners and saints, it reminds us that the seemingly godless often dwell closest to God, and those who seem godly often get it just as wrong as everyone else. It was into such a world that our Savior was born, and it is to such people that he proclaimed salvation. The dissonance we find in Rahab's narrative echoes the dissonance of Advent.

This dissonance strikes the attentive reader as soon as Joshua 2 opens with the people of Israel encamped at place called Shittim (Joshua 2:1). Numbers 25 tells us that while they were at Shittim, the people of Israel "made themselves impure by having illicit sex with Moabite women" (Numbers 25:1). The word for "illicit sex" is closely related to the Hebrew word for "prostitute" or "prostitution," and the story eventually ended with Israelite idolatry and divine wrath. Thus, the mention of Shittim in Joshua 2 hints that something bad lay on the horizon. Astute readers might get a déjà vu feeling, especially when the men Joshua sends to investigate Jericho "just so happen" to end up in the house of a prostitute, of all people (Joshua 2:1).

Even this prostitute's name, Rahab, may have evoked provocative images and urges. The word *rahab* means "wide, broad, or open" in Hebrew, and the verb means "to open," which may have carried sexual connotations. In Ugaritic, a related language, *rahab* can refer to female sexual organs. And the Babylonian Talmud, a later Jewish body of literature, says that the very mention of Rahab's name could cause the speaker sexual arousal.[2] At the mention of Rahab's name, men gathered around a military campfire might have smirked as if a smutty anecdote were about to be shared. In other words, the spies from Joshua find themselves in a sex-saturated joke. They walk right into it with their eyes wide shut and "bedded down there" (Joshua 2:1), an expression that is often a Hebrew euphemism for sex. Two unnamed soldiers in the home of a prostitute does not stretch the imagination. It becomes worse when we recognize that they know of Jericho's impending conquest—Rahab is one of the enemies the Israelites are about to destroy. These soldiers, then, intend to use her and to throw her away with the rest of Jericho. They hardly represent godliness and moral purity. The symbolism of the Israelites encamping at Shittim proves quite appropriate.

Yet, in contrast to these two foolish soldiers, of whom we should expect so much more, the Gentile prostitute Rahab, like Tamar, proves more righteous than her male, Israelite counterparts. In fact, because of her exceeding righteousness, which the narrator will soon reveal, many interpreters through the centuries have questioned whether or not Rahab really worked as a prostitute. Whitewashing her story, they have spoken of Rahab as a landlord, an innkeeper, or a simple business woman (in charge of imports and exports, maybe?).[3] Surely God would not use a prostitute, right?

Wrong.

The crux of the plot lies precisely in setting up the contrast between these men from a holy people and this woman whose profession suggests she is immoral. Rahab has three strikes against her: First, she is a Canaanite. Second, she is a female. And third, she is a prostitute. In a patriarchal, pro-Israelite worldview that prized sexual morality, Rahab was the ultimate outsider. Nevertheless, herein we may see something about the character of God. No woman chooses the profession of prostitution because she enjoys it. No little girl grows up wanting sell her body. No daddy wants that for his daughter. Yet, without job prospects and the harsh realities of economic stress weighing on the family, "women like [Rahab] sometimes found themselves on the edge of life, with slavery or prostitution their only options. If that is the assumption of the story's author and audience, then Rahab's role as prostitute may actually foster sympathy for her."[4] This ultimate outsider received God's sympathy, even if she did not receive the sympathy of the two male spies. The rest of the story bears that out, as even Rahab finds a place among the chosen people of God.

A Bold Confession

The comedic awkwardness of the situation—two spies who begin their mission by going straight to a prostitute's house—continues to escalate when someone tells the king of Jericho about them. The king, predictably, sends his messengers to Rahab's house to find the spies, but Rahab had already hidden them on her roof. We should imagine here a scene resembling something out of an American sitcom—as when a teenage boy has slipped into a teenage girl's bedroom, and when the dad comes knocking on the door, the boy is hidden precariously under the bed. Early readers and hearers of this story would have laughed not only at the thought of sexually aroused soldiers hiding on the roof of Rahab's house, but also of a prostitute so easily deceiving officials from the king.

We might imagine her batting her eyes as she tells them, "Of course the men came to me. But I didn't know where they were from. The men left when it was time to close the gate at dark, but I don't know where the men went. Hurry! Chase after them! You might catch up with them" (Joshua 2:4-5). Unquestioningly accepting the story of the woman in front of them, the king's messengers follow her false trail and leave the city in pursuit of the spies. Yet again, "the underdog, a female 'prostitute' leaves men searching in vain."[5] Closing the gate behind them, the king's messengers unwittingly lock the Israelite spites in the city, making the spies even more dependent on the goodwill and hospitality of Rahab.

However, when she arrives on the roof where she hid them, Joshua's spies receive more than just the goodwill and hospitality of this Canaanite prostitute. They receive a word of verification and a religious confession that rivals the theology of Moses himself:

> She said to the men, "I know that the LORD has given you the land. Terror over you has overwhelmed us. The entire population of the land has melted down in fear because of you. We have heard how the LORD dried up the water of the Reed Sea in front of you when you left Egypt. We have also heard what you did to Sihon and Og, the two kings of the Amorites on the other side of the Jordan. You utterly wiped them out. We heard this and our hearts turned to water. Because of you, people can no longer work up their courage. This is because the LORD your God is God in heaven above and on earth below. (Joshua 2:9-11)

This confession of a Canaanite prostitute—not the Israelite spies!—is the central, most significant religious assertion of this entire story, if not the entire Book of Joshua. These words come from the mouth of this unexpected source; God chooses to encourage God's people through the mouth of a morally and religiously suspect woman. This tells us not only the degree to which God is committed to Israel, but also that God has good purposes for the Canaanites, too.

From the mouth of a Canaanite prostitute, we receive arguably the best theology of the entire Book of Joshua. From her, we receive the confirmation that God has, indeed, given Israel this land, despite Israel's doubt (the reason they sent the spies in). From her, we hear the confirmation that God intends to bring this plan about through God's own power and sovereignty, not merely Israel's military might.[6] From her, a member of a polytheistic culture, we hear the affirmation that the one God of Israel truly exercises authority "in heaven above and on earth below" (2:11), that is, "over all spheres of existence."[7] Indeed, from her lips, we hear about the total destruction of Israel's enemies across the Jordan (2:10), which contains this book's first reference to the theological concept of total destruction devoted to God.[8] A fair amount of irony hangs in the air here when these theological affirmations, from top to bottom, do not come from the Israelite spies or even from Joshua, but from the mouth of a woman, the mouth of a Canaanite, the mouth of a prostitute.

Still, Rahab does not stop with mere theological affirmations designed to boost the spies' confidence. From her confession, she then makes an ethical request: "Now, I have been loyal to you. So pledge to me by the LORD that you in turn will deal loyally with my family. Give me a sign of good faith. Spare the lives of my father, mother, brothers, and sisters, along with everything they own. Rescue us from death" (Joshua 2:12-13).

The foundation of this appeal has two components. First, she appeals to them "by the LORD." By bringing God's name into the mix, she asks the Israelite spies to act in accordance with the revealed character of their God—a God who has, throughout history, shown a preferential option for the powerless. Second, Rahab grounds the appeal in her own act of hospitality, counting on an ancient near eastern ethic that places a high value on hospitality. By that standard, the spies should act like family toward her because she has acted like family toward them. Usually such a request for family-like protection can be made only between actual *family* or members of the same tribe.[9] But as a woman who has shown herself theologically astute and pragmatically valuable, she believes the boldness of this treat-me-like-family request has warrant.

The spies know theological problems abound with this request. To make such an agreement with the one of the Canaanites violates the clear rules Moses gave Israel not to make covenants with the people of the land because "it will become a dangerous trap for you" (Exodus 23:33). In short, Rahab's request not only violates the law of God, which serves as the basis of Israel's claim to the land (see Joshua 1:6-8), but it also invites all kinds of moral and religious chaos. Nevertheless, despite these serious concerns, the spies have no firm footing for negotiation. Whether they respect her theology or not—whether they appreciate her protection or not—as long as they find themselves hiding in her house, they must live by her rules. As one scholar writes, "on her rooftop, beneath a pile of flax, in a place where their movement might be detected by Rahab's neighbors, the spies are at Rahab's mercy."[10] Predictably, then, they give in to the one option they have and enter into this agreement, this covenant, with Rahab: "We swear by our own lives to secure yours. If you don't reveal our mission, we will deal loyally and faithfully with you when the LORD gives us the land" (Joshua 2:14).

Protecting Rahab

With their promise of protection in place, Rahab reveals the escape route to the Israelite spies. Her house, built literally within the protective walls of the city, has window access to the outside world. Handing them a rope, she instructs them to lower themselves out of the window and into freedom. Only then, once they know how to escape, do the spies try to turn the tables on her a bit. Showing their true character, once again contrasted with Rahab's, they make it seem as if she forced them into the promise they just made, speaking of "this pledge you *made* us swear" (2:17, emphasis mine). Because they feel forced into their current situation, and because they now know how to escape, they begin to add new stipulations to the covenant they made with Rahab. In order for her family to be saved, they must all be present in her home at the time of the attack. Any family members not in Rahab's home will suffer the fate of the rest of the city.

The spies also ask Rahab to tie a red cord outsider her window on the day of the attack (Joshua 2:18). Jewish tradition has often connected this cord with the blood placed on the doorposts on the night the angel of death passed over Egypt (Exodus 12:7), specifically paralleling that blood's protective quality.[11] If this connection has merit, the narrator echoes the Passover story in describing the rescue of a *Canaanite* family. This speaks, again, to the character of God. The God of Israel is not concerned only with rescuing Israel. Rather, God's intention lies in rescuing all of creation, all the nations of the earth. God invites all the peoples of the earth, from Jerusalem to Jericho, to participate in the salvation that so many have thought restricted to one people, Israel. God's ultimate intention, even for the Canaanites, does not lie in destruction, but in Exodus-like liberation.

Tying the red cord to her window, Rahab agrees to the stipulations of the spies. The spies wait for three days and return to Joshua with the good news—news delivered in a nearly word for word reflection of Rahab's confession: "The Lord has definitely given the entire land into our power. In addition, all of the land's population has melted down in fear because of us" (2:24). The words of the Canaanite prostitute become the trumpet call for all Israel, including Joshua, to enter into the Promised Land. The first spy mission to Canaan in Numbers 13 yielded disheartening reports and produced utter lack of faith in Israel. This time, inspired by a Canaanite prostitute, the spies have full confidence in the power of Israel's God.[12] God has, quite literally, given Israel a second chance to respond in faith.

It takes four more chapters before we learn the fate of Jericho and Rahab. In Joshua 6, the narrator tells us of the fall of the walls of Jericho through shouts and trumpets of Israel's army. This confirms the reality that Rahab voiced: The Israelites' conquest of the land comes about by God's sovereignty, not by their military might. We also learn that the Israelites destroyed every single person in the city (Joshua 6:21). But we also find that Joshua and the Israelites maintain the agreement with Rahab, protecting her and her family (Joshua 6:17, 22-23). Despite Moses' laws prohibiting the protection of Canaanite life during entrance into the land (Deuteronomy 20:16-18), Israel has reciprocated Rahab's hospitality toward the spies. And so, we read, Rahab's family "still lives among Israel today" (Joshua 6:25). In the inclusion of Rahab and her family, we see that God's ultimate desire is not exclusion but embrace; not rejection but reception; not destruction but liberation.

Rahab's inclusion among the people of God shows that the defining factor for acceptance is neither ethnic identity nor moral uprightness, but faith that responds to God's activity in the world. In her expression of faith she is, like Tamar, more righteous than the people who assumed religious privilege due to their ethnic heritage. Whereas the people of promise act promiscuously (both literally and spiritually), this Canaanite prostitute becomes an inspiration for Israel's faithfulness. Though Israel has the word of God at their disposal, Rahab's conviction and conduct more accurately reflects that word. Though Israel has the divine commands, Rahab's actions exhibit a more careful response to the heart of God. Though destructive power of war dominates the larger plot of Joshua, the faith of a Canaanite prostitute stands out in the subplot and calls into question the clean and ordered world of moral black and white. The Canaanites that live among the people of God throughout time are not objects to be destroyed, but gifts of the God who is revealed to the world through the most unexpected people.

God is revealed to the world through unexpected people. That's an Advent message If ever there was one. Who, after all, could be more unexpected than the son of a carpenter born in Bethlehem? And this is Matthew's message when he includes Rahab and these other women in his genealogy of the Messiah. A God who has, throughout Israel's story, been revealed *through Gentiles* desires nothing more than to extend the divine message of salvation to those same Gentiles. In the Advent season, most of the world prepares for Christmas by gathering together with people just like ourselves. But the story of Rahab reminds us that God has always worked in the lives of people different from us. The people we tend to overlook or even reject might very well be the means by which God speaks to us. "Throughout the Bible and church history, God has opened new doors and new opportunities for his people through the most unlikely people."[13] Advent affords us yet another opportunity to reflect on the inclusion of those unlike us in the family of God. Advent affords us yet another opportunity to invite these others to sit around our table with all the rights and privileges of *family*.

Rahab Gives Us a New Perspective

We cannot end our discussion of Rahab without addressing the very important topic of God and violence in the Bible. How can the One who accepts outsiders into God's family also destroy their family? This question lies at the heart of many people's objections to the Christian faith. But once we grant that the writer of Joshua actually cares about the subject as well, we can see in the Rahab story his attempt to wrestle with it. Through this wrestling, the writer of Joshua resists accepting blindly the destruction commands of Deuteronomy. He has little interest in just promoting an ideology of destruction or a politically motivated theology of occupation. By placing the greatest religious confession of the book on the lips of a Canaanite prostitute, the writer of Joshua intends to show us the openness of God to the faithful responses of the Canaanites. Indeed, not only the responses of the *confessing* Canaanites, but even an openness to the family members of Rahab who, themselves, expressed no faith in Israel's God.

This is not to say that the writer of Joshua holds a pacifist position or didn't condone some violence. He absolutely did. But the function of the Rahab story is to set a sharp contrast between the supposedly righteous Israelites, who act in doubt and promiscuity, and the supposedly unrighteous Canaanites, at least one of whom acted faithfully. Since the world cannot be so easily divided between the good guys and the bad guys, this story does not support blind and unthinking calls to violence. Rahab's story warns us that the world cannot be divided into nice, clean, moral and religious "us versus them" categories. All people, even those we deem enemies, should be viewed in light of their God-given worth and their potential to be agents of God's grace in the world. The world will not ultimately be judged based on tribes, ethnicities, denominations, political affiliations, or national identification, but solely and completely based on the shed blood of the Messiah, Jesus, who has within his own family tree these unexpected, righteous underdogs and outsiders. In this, violence and genocide do not win. Grace wins. It always has. It always will. That is another Advent message for us, as we prepare to welcome the Prince of Peace.

This promise of grace's ultimate victory carries me on each day as I think about my family's destiny. God did not send the Son into a perfect family, filled with perfect people, who didn't need saving to begin with. God sent the Messiah into a family like mine. Overly pious saints of a holier-than-thou church may look at my family and see rebels destined to destruction. But when I look at my family, I see Rahab. Which means I see the divine possibility of hearing an unexpected, world-altering word from God from any one of my family members at any moment—words that save, just as Rahab's words saved.

Questions for Reflection and Discussion

1. Reread Rahab's words in Joshua 2:9-11. What does it mean that such a significant theological statement came from a Canaanite and prostitute? How does this shape your understanding of God, and the people through whom God works?

2. Have you ever heard God speak to you from an unexpected, even "unholy" source? What did God say, and what did you learn? Why do you think God spoke to you in that way?

3. When was the last time you gave someone outside your family the privileges of family? Have you ever considered doing this for your enemies? What do you think would happen if you did? What fears do you have about such an invitation?

4. We live in a time when questioning those who wield the power of the sword can incur the wrath of our neighbors

and family. Why do you think it matters to Joshua's writer to question the violence in the book through the Rahab story? What do you think it cost him?

5. What do you think it would cost you to be the kind of person who doesn't allow yourself or others to default to violence on interpersonal or national levels?

6. What are some practical things you can do in your family, workplace, or church to begin talking about our enemies differently, so that we can see them as people created in the image of God? What are some specific things you can stop saying, or start saying? What are assumptions it might be time for you to challenge?

7. How do you see in Rahab a glimpse of the hope of Advent?

Prayer

Father of Rahab, teach us to see our enemies through your eyes and with your grace. Remind us that your love does not run out once it hits the threshold of our churches or our nation, but extends to even the most foreign and offensive person to us. Let us not give in to the temptations to divide your world too easily between insiders and outsiders, but let us embrace the ambiguities of reality that you came to seek and save sinners, of whom we are the worst.

Focus for the Week

The contrast between Rahab and the Israelite spies, between the place of ill repute in which they hide and between the prostitute's confession of faith, is as humorous as it is holy. In this situation, we see the smut and sanctity of the world come together. Joshua's spies heard a profound theological witness from an unlikely source. When we open our eyes to see the work of God, we open ourselves to a world where the word becomes flesh in ways we never anticipated.

This week, take an opportunity to listen for God's voice in a place you normally would not expect. When your family member tries to talk to you about religion, give him or her your time. When your coworker begins musing positively or negatively on religious things, fan the flame of the conversation. When a non-Christian speaks about God, choose to listen rather than dismiss him or interject your own thoughts. Maybe even approach a long-time enemy and apologize for your piece of the broken relationship, making it known to them that you believe in a God who reconciles enemies. Who knows, you may be surprised at what such a confession would do in the life of your enemy—they might even play a role in saving your soul!

---

1. From *Joshua: Interpretation, a Bible Commentary for Teaching and Preaching*, by Jerome F. D. Creach (Westminster John Knox Press, 2012); page 42.

2. From *Joshua: Interpretation, a Bible Commentary for Teaching and Preaching*, by Jerome F. D. Creach (Westminster John Knox Press, 2012); page 32.

3. From *Joshua: Interpretation, a Bible Commentary for Teaching and Preaching*, by Jerome F. D. Creach (Westminster John Knox Press, 2012); page 33.

4. From *Joshua: Interpretation, a Bible Commentary for Teaching and Preaching*, by Jerome F. D. Creach (Westminster John Knox Press, 2012); pages 33–34.

5. From *Mothers on the Margins?: The Significance of Women in Matthew's Genealogy*, by E. Anne Clements (Pickwick Publications, 2014); page 74.

6. From *Mothers on the Margins?: The Significance of Women in Matthew's Genealogy*, by E. Anne Clements (Pickwick Publications, 2014); page 75.

7. From *Joshua: Word Biblical Commentary*, Volume 7, by Trent C. Butler (Word Books, 1983); page 33.

8. From *Mothers on the Margins?: The Significance of Women in Matthew's Genealogy*, by E. Anne Clements (Pickwick Publications, 2014); page 75.

9. From *Mothers on the Margins?: The Significance of Women in Matthew's Genealogy*, by E. Anne Clements (Pickwick Publications, 2014); page 77.

10. From *Joshua: Interpretation, a Bible Commentary for Teaching and Preaching,* by Jerome F. D. Creach (Westminster John Knox Press, 2012), page 34.

11. From *Joshua: Interpretation, a Bible Commentary for Teaching and Preaching,* by Jerome F. D. Creach (Westminster John Knox Press, 2012); page 37.

12. From *Mothers on the Margins?: The Significance of Women in Matthew's Genealogy,* by E. Anne Clements (Pickwick Publications, 2014); page 79.

13. From *Joshua: Word Biblical Commentary,* Volume 7, by Trent C. Butler (Word Books, 1983); pages 34–35.

CHAPTER 3

Ruth
The Lady in Waiting

Key Scripture: The Book of Ruth

The third woman Matthew names in his genealogy of Jesus is Ruth, which points us to her story in the Old Testament book named after her. Ruth's story captures our Advent hope and prepares us for Christ as it lifts up a vision of unexpected, sacrificial love.

For my part, I've had a long, torrid love affair with Ruth. Way back in high school, I knew the person who would become my wife, but she had no interest in dating me. I began to write her love letters (masked in friendship) about the forbidden love between Baptists. I went to a Fundamentalist Baptist church and she attended a Southern Baptist church, which for us meant that we couldn't date. In my letters, I drew parallels between our forbidden love and the forbidden love between the Moabite Ruth and the Israelite Boaz. I wrote to my eventual wife of the ways Boaz and Ruth took care of each other, responded to each other's needs, wooed each other, protected each other, and lived within—and sometimes outside of—the rules that governed larger Israelite morality. Again, she had no interest in me at the time, but I had convinced myself that this young lady had marriage potential. I *would* be her Boaz, and she *would* be my Ruth.

Undoubtedly, with the rudimentary biblical interpretation skills I had as a high schooler, I butchered the point, meaning, and purpose of the Book of Ruth. Still, I knew one thing clearly: If nothing else, Ruth concerns itself with unlawful, unorthodox, and unexpected love. Whether addressing the love between an Israelite woman (Naomi) and her Moabite daughter-in-law (Ruth), or the love that develops between the Israelite Boaz and the foreigner Ruth, this book shows a host of self-sacrificing, self-giving relationships of intentional affection that lie outside the cultural norms of its day.

These relationships do not exist against a neutral backdrop. The Book of Ruth is set during the time of the judges (1200–1000 B.C.), but most scholars suspect the author penned Ruth around the same time as Ezra and Nehemiah were written (fifth to fourth centuries B.C.). Both of these books express strong disapproval of Israelites intermarrying with foreigners (Ezra 9:10-12; Nehemiah 10:30; 13:23-27). The Book of Ezra goes so far as to suggest that Israelites who have married and had children with foreign women ought to *divorce their wives* and completely separate themselves from the foreigners around them (Ezra 10:10-11). In these books, marrying foreign women threatens Israel's identity. With such a background in mind, we can see how the Book of Ruth's depiction of a righteous Moabite woman might seem counterintuitive and scandalous. In a time when national identity stands in question, a book celebrating marriage to a foreigner raises all kinds of problems. Ruth challenges all the "us versus them" categories that make people feel secure in their identity.

As if that were not enough, this book raises up two female main characters. Aside from the Book of Esther, no other book of the Bible features women to the degree Ruth does. As one scholar writes, in a world dominated by men,

"Ruth is a daring model of a woman who acts decisively to create a future for herself in a patriarchal social context where no good future was on offer for her."[1] As we saw in Chapter 1, vulnerable women in Israelite society had few good options. Social Security and Medicare did not yet exist. No one had yet dreamt up women's shelters, welfare, or charity organizations for widowed women. And we can forget about job opportunities. But Ruth finds a way to secure herself and her mother-in-law Naomi despite these challenges.

Yet, even more spectacularly, Ruth does all these daring, faithful, self-sacrificing acts with very little reference to the God of Israel. God never once speaks to her or appears to her in the story, and only twice does the LORD act directly in the whole book (Ruth 1:6 and 4:13).[2] Ruth exhibits an admirable moral character, but her actions of self-giving love come out of a sincere heart of compassion, not a heart given over to the God whose people in the period of Judges look eerily like the Canaanites. Nevertheless, we cannot assume God does not act throughout Ruth's story. Like in Esther, the God who rarely acts overtly and objectively seems quite active in the background, working through human deeds to bring about the good divine plan. We cannot assume absence on the part of God. Rather, God chooses to work in this book in ways we would not expect—through a Moabite woman's everyday acts of goodness. We should not expect flash and bang with this story, but if we can open our eyes, we will see God's fingerprints in the unexciting actions and lives of faithful, good people who treat each other with simple kindness, respect, and love, despite their differences.

We see this faithfulness in all three main characters in this account—Ruth, Naomi, and Boaz—held in contrast to the other members of Israelite society. Ruth 1:1 tells us that this story takes place "during the days when the judges ruled." This brief historical marker in a story dominated by two women reminds us of how, in the period of the judges,

Israel constantly fought against foreigners and routinely treated women inhumanely (see Judges 11:29-40; 19; 21). The goodness of the characters in Ruth stands out sharply against the picture of Israel we see at the end of Judges, in which the tribes are struggling to find their moral way.

Those Naughty Moabites

The story of these individuals' affection for one another begins in famine rather than flourishing. A man named Elimelech, along with his wife Naomi and their two sons, moves to Moab after their crops fail in Bethlehem (Ruth 1:1-2). Then crisis follows crisis. Noami's husband Elimelech dies, and after they have married Moabite women, both of Naomi's sons also die (Ruth 1:3-5). Naomi now finds herself having fallen from a position of security for a woman in the ancient world (wife and mother of sons) to one of the most destitute positions in the ancient world (a widow with no sons). Her husband took her to a foreign land, her sons married foreign women, and then all three men up and died. It was as if they abandoned her to live among foreigners.

But these were not just any foreigners, they were some of the *worst* foreigners: Moabites. In the Hebrew Scriptures, the Moabites frequently play the part of the "bad guys." The Moabite nation began from an incestuous relationship between Lot and his daughters (Genesis 19:29-38). Later a Moabite king hired a foreign prophet to curse the Israelites, though he was unsuccessful (Numbers 22–24). When the people intermarried with the Moabites on their way to the Promised Land, the Moabites convinced them to worship their god, contributing to a compromised faith and moral chaos among God's people (Numbers 25:1-5). In short, in Israel's imagination all Moabites fall under the moniker of incestuous, inhospitable, idolatrous foreigners. Moabite women, however, get the added descriptor of temptresses.

But, as we shall see, Ruth defies the stereotype. None of those adjectives apply to her.

We immediately see that Ruth has pleased her mother-in-law. Before they died, Naomi's sons married Ruth and Orpah (Ruth 1:4). Naomi shows deep respect for the character of her two Moabite daughters-in-law, yet she knows that with the loss of her husband and sons, she cannot provide for these women. She tries to send them back to their homeland, families, and gods. After all, what has serving Israel's God gotten Naomi except the feeling of abandonment (1:13) and resultant bitterness (1:20)?

After initially refusing, Orpah eventually goes back to her homeland. But Ruth resolves to stay with Naomi (Ruth 1:8-18). Given this situation, we ought not blame Orpah for returning to her family. Naomi certainly does not blame her. Yet, given the hopeless situation, Orpah's return makes Ruth's commitment all the more impressive. In beautiful words, often read in Christian weddings for some reason, Ruth commits herself to her mother-in-law: "Wherever you go, I will go; and wherever you stay, I will stay. Your people will be my people, and your God will be my God. Wherever you die, I will die, and there I will be buried. May the LORD do this to me and more if even death separates me from you" (Ruth 1:16-17). She does this not because that woman can offer her anything, and not because that woman can eventually gain her a husband, but simply because Ruth has exceptional character. "With extraordinary devotion, she forfeits the security of her homeland and joins her fate to a woman with no prospects."[3]

Your People Will Be My People, and Your God Will Be My God

The kind of commitment Ruth proposes to Naomi reflects Israelite teachings on the character of God. Her reaffirmation of commitment to Naomi as her only family reflects God's familial commitment to Israel. Indeed, Ruth's active, self-giving affection for Naomi parallels the qualities Israel reveres most about God, especially the "acts of unexpected and unmerited grace and mercy . . . the giving of more than could ever be earned or deserved."[4] What could Naomi ever say in response to such God-like self-giving? Nothing. She simply accepts Ruth's loyalty, and they move on to Bethlehem together. Naomi feels bitter and empty, instructing those around her to call her *Mara*, meaning bitter (Ruth 1:20). But neither Ruth nor the narrator accepts this assessment as the final word. In fact, the narrator refuses to even call her Mara"(bitter), despite Naomi's request, foreshadowing that this bitterness does not ultimately have the final say. The transformation of her circumstances and disposition will come about through Ruth.

While the narrator refuses to call Naomi Mara, he does not cease to call Ruth a Moabite (Ruth 2:2). Naomi's fullness and wellness must come through a Moabite or not at all. Ruth's status as a Moabite does not just create potential religious problems when they arrive back in Bethlehem. The very fact of her foreign status puts Ruth at risk of rape or murder as she takes one of the only options available: rummaging through the left-over grain in the fields of Israelite farmers (Ruth 2:2). A poor, foreign, single woman working alone in the fields was vulnerable to assault. We should not imagine that Israelite men were less violent than other men just because they have Israelite heritage. The period of the judges has few respectable male heroes and a large number of victimized women. A Moabite woman working among men in a grain field spells potential disaster.

Nevertheless, Ruth's willingness to go out into these dangerous grain fields to get food for Naomi shows, again, her radical commitment to this older woman. This commitment catches the eye of a local landowner, Boaz, who then inquiries about Ruth's identity. The answer he receives tells him all he needs to know about Ruth's character: "She's a young Moabite woman, the one who returned with Naomi from the territory of Moab. She said, 'Please let me glean so that I might gather up grain from among the bundles behind the harvesters.' She arrived and has been on her feet from the morning until now, and has sat down for only a moment" (Ruth 2:6-7). Nothing would surprise an Israelite man more than a Moabite woman tirelessly working on behalf of another helpless human being.

Though Boaz's expression of affection for Ruth cannot rival the poetic quality of Ruth's words of affection for Naomi in 1:16-17, his concrete actions convey a commitment just as deep. He approaches Ruth and instructs her to continue gleaning in his field with his young women. He orders his men to leave her alone, thus protecting her from potential assault, and offers her water whenever she is thirsty (Ruth 2:8-9). Nothing required Boaz to offer this kindness, protecting her from hunger, thirst, and would-be rapists or thieves.[5] Yet he did it anyway.

Obviously confused by this proliferation of protection and favor, Ruth immediately asks why he would express such generosity given his awareness of her foreign ancestry (Ruth 2:10). Boaz's response to this question reveals the depth of his respect for her. He sees her, really, as an Abraham-like figure:

> Boaz responded to her, "Everything that you did for your mother-in-law after your husband's death has been reported fully to me: how you left behind your father, your mother, and the land of your birth, and came to a people you hadn't known beforehand. [12] May the LORD reward you for your deed. May you receive a rich reward from the LORD, the God of Israel, under whose wings you've come to seek refuge. (Ruth 2:11-12)

Like Abraham, Ruth abandoned father and mother to go live in a foreign land with people she did not know (Genesis 12:1-4). Only unlike Abraham, she did all this "with no possession, no family, no call of God, and no promise of any blessings."[6] Due to her extraordinary faithfulness to Naomi, Boaz invokes the faithful God to respond to her in kind.

Indeed, more than that, Boaz shows himself to be the willing *means* by which God's kindness pours out on Ruth. Boaz refuses to see a sister in need and only say, "Go in peace! Stay warm! Have a nice meal!" (James 2:16). No, he provides for her protection, invites her to dine with him, and even sends her back home with an abundance of provision (Ruth 2:14-17). Even Naomi cannot deny the hand of God in Boaz's generosity (2:20).

Risky Plan

The arrival of Boaz on the scene becomes the pivotal moment for Naomi and Ruth. In the ancient form of playing match-maker, Naomi takes steps to bring Boaz and Ruth together in marriage. She figures out the specific formula for the highest compatibility, telling Ruth how to blindside Boaz with a blind date: "Now isn't Boaz, whose young women you were with, our relative? Tonight he will be winnowing barley at the threshing floor. You should bathe, put on some perfume, wear nice clothes, and then go down to the threshing floor. Don't make yourself known to the man until he has finished eating and drinking. When he lies down, notice the place where he is lying. Then go, uncover his feet, and lie down. And he will tell you what to do" (Ruth 3:2-4). The instructions Naomi provides here are the preparations a bride might make on her wedding day in Israelite culture. Naomi and Ruth are on the prowl for a husband.

Naomi identifies a time when Ruth can approach Boaz, when he will be "in a good mood" after eating and drinking— relaxed, happy, and possibly drunk (Ruth 3:3, 7). Her instructions for Ruth contain numerous sexual euphemisms in the Hebrew: "make yourself known" ("know" often meant "have sex with"); "lie down" (also a reference to sex);

"uncover" (a reference to removing clothing); and "his feet" (a reference to the genitals).[7] These euphemistic references may seem out of place in the Bible, but the original hearers of this story undoubtedly would have caught the double-entendre. Naomi is instructing Ruth to have a possibly sexual, certainly risqué encounter with Boaz in the middle of the night.

The good daughter-in-law promises to obey Naomi by submitting herself to the instructions of Boaz. Waiting for Boaz to drink himself into a slumber, she approaches him as Naomi tutored. Startled out of his sleep because the presence of a strange woman at his "feet," Boaz asks about her identity for the second time in the story. The first time, Boaz's worker gave him the down-low of her identity as a nameless Moabite accompanying Naomi (Ruth 2:6-7), but this time Ruth gets to speak for herself, first by asserting her name and then by noting his responsibilities toward her: "I'm Ruth your servant. Spread out your robe over your servant, because you are a redeemer" (3:9). By stating her name—in contrast to Boaz's servant who speaks of her only as "a young Moabite woman"—Ruth indicates her individual identity as distinct from the stereotypes about other Moabites.

The narrator of this story has set up this contrast between Ruth and other Moabites from the beginning. For original hearers of this story, Ruth the Moabite approaching Boaz on the threshing floor unmistakably echoed the story of Lot and his daughters at the end of Genesis 19. In Genesis 19, Lot's daughters get their father drunk and sleep with him so that they can have children. The Moabite and Ammonite people were products of this incestuous affair. Both stories, then, involve a man passed out drunk and a woman desperate for sons and a future trying to take advantage of him. The difference, however, lies in the fact that Ruth, unlike her foremothers, does not essentially rape Boaz, as Lot's daughters did their father. She states her name, clearly making known her identity rather than hiding it. She seeks Boaz in a vulnerable state, but does not exploit him or manipulate him. She asks, makes her availability known, and then lets him choose. Earlier in the story, Boaz recognized that Ruth had come seeking refuge under God's wings, and prayed that the LORD would reward her (Ruth 2:12). Now Ruth calls in that prayer by asking Boaz to spread his wings, or robe, over her and become the mechanism of God's protection (Ruth 3:9). In other words, she asks him to "redeem" her, and he readily agrees.

Because we have overused and underappreciated the word "redeem" in the Christian tradition, we fail to comprehend Ruth's request. "To redeem" in the Hebrew does not carry primarily religious overtones. Rather, as Sandra Richter observes, the term conveys financial meaning:

> So what are the practical expressions of Boaz agreeing to redeem this young woman? As the story unfolds, we see that "to redeem" in this situation means that Boaz will marry Ruth, buy back the patrimony of her deceased husband (cf. the inalienable land law of Lev 25), take both Ruth and Naomi into his household, and father a child in Mahlon's name, thereby giving Elimelech an heir to whom the family inheritance will pass (cf. the levirate law of Deut 25) . . . the tribal law of "redemption" had to do with a patriarch rescuing a family member who, due to crippling life circumstances, had been lost to the kinship circle, to protect their legal rights. The law demanded that the patriarch protect the individual's legal rights and resolve her debts. Here is a reconciliation of family ties that costs the redeemer. And it is the oldest, closest male relative to whom one looks for help and hope.[8]

Indeed, herein lies the problem going forward. Boaz knows that another, closer male relative actually has claim on Elimelech's property and, therefore, on the responsibility to redeem Ruth. Sending Ruth back to Naomi with more than enough provision, Boaz sets up a meeting with this nearer relative and ten witnesses. He tells him,

> Naomi, who has returned from the field of Moab, is selling
> the portion of the field that belonged to our brother
> Elimelech. I thought that I should let you know and say,
> "Buy it, in the presence of those sitting here and in the
> presence of the elders of my people." If you will redeem it,
> redeem it; but if you won't redeem it, tell me so that I may
> know. There isn't anyone to redeem it except you, and I'm
> next in line after you. (Ruth 4:3-4)

Clearly, in this opening statement Boaz has not revealed
the whole of Elimelech's estate, as he has said nothing
about Ruth. But, as a shrewd business man, he appears to
have made this a part of his ploy. As soon as the other man
says, "I'll take it," referring to the land, Boaz then slips
in the bit about Ruth: "On the day that you buy the field
from Naomi, you also buy Ruth the Moabite, the wife of the
dead man, in order to preserve the dead man's name for his
inheritance" (Ruth 4:5).

This new bit of information changes the entire game
for the closer relative. Just as Onan in the story of Tamar
looked primarily to protect his own family's inheritance
(Genesis 38:9), this fellow understands that purchasing
this land could ultimately end up in a loss for him. Why
put his family's fortune at stake to purchase land that
could ultimately hurt his financial security because of
the presence of a Moabite? Why purchase this land just
to potentially hand it over in the name of Naomi's son,
Mahlon? This transaction seems pointless after hearing
of the Ruth addendum. Since this man does not have the
same familial obligation as did Onan in the Tamar story,
he can back out of the deal without losing face. He takes
off his sandal and hands it over to Boaz, before witnesses,
as a symbol of the fact that he has transferred the rights
of redemption over to Boaz. In this action, he forfeits any
claim on Elimelech's property, wife, or daughter-in-law.

Now Boaz can rightfully and legally step up.
Understanding the risks to his own finances that come
along with marrying Ruth, he marries her anyway, and

in the birth of her firstborn son, Boaz provides an heir for Naomi and guarantees that Elimelech's lineage does not die. The key in this, however, is not merely the fact that Boaz did this, but the *reason* he did this. As Helen Pearson writes, "Boaz claimed his covenant responsibility for Naomi's family, not because the law demanded it but because loving-kindness . . . demanded it."[9] Boaz provided the answer to his own prayers on behalf of Ruth.

God Steps Up

Through Boaz's action, God stepped up: "The LORD let [Ruth] become pregnant, and she gave birth to a son" (Ruth 4:13). The overtly-stated, direct action of God comes at the end, once all the human actors in the story have done their best. Recognizing the blessings of the God of Israel, Ruth continues to keep her promises to Naomi by staying faithful and providing a future for her. Even Naomi, so pessimistic and empty in the beginning of the story, cannot help but see the hand of God these happenings, and the women around her confess their belief as well: "May the Lord be blessed, who today hasn't left you without a redeemer. May his name be proclaimed in Israel. He will restore your life and sustain you in your old age. Your daughter-in-law who loves you has given birth to him. She's better for you than seven sons" (Ruth 4:14-15).

And, indeed, their prayer is answered, Naomi's grandson's name will be great, as the genealogy at the end of the story indicates. This child, Obed, became the father of Jesse, who then fathered David. The Book of Ruth began in the dark shadow of the Book of Judges, with famine and death dominating the landscape. But it ends with a genealogy—a possibility of hope, life, and a future for the faithful. The greatest king of Israel, and the great Messiah of Israel, came from the womb of a poor Moabite woman most people overlooked and underestimated.

This woman, Ruth, and the cast of characters around her, refused to rely passively on prayer and providence. Their willingness to get things rolling, push the boundaries, question dominant assumptions, and see life in the faces of those who are different provided the fertile ground through which God wove a tapestry of redemption. The world improves when Christians who pray also realize God sometimes calls us to serve as the answer to our own prayers, as Boaz did. The world looks better when Christians are willing to challenge our own stereotypes about our nation's enemies and welcome them into our homes, provide for their protection, and eat meals with them. In a world like the world of Judges, where everyone wants to argue about international conflict—or in a world of nuclear bombs and drones—we cannot avoid the call of the Book of Ruth to stop avoiding our enemies and start figuring out how to make them *family*.

But this family-making does not exclusively happen in big, dramatic acts. Without a willingness to do the little things and develop the habits the create characters of faithfulness and hospitality, we should never expect to find ourselves performing big acts of faithfulness. The Book of Ruth reminds us that some of the most important movements of redemptive history do not look miraculous or remarkable. Rather, often "the symptoms and effects of the life of faith are totally unspectacular,"[10] like pledges of faithfulness, traveling with another woman without male protection, providing meals for the underprivileged, and commonplace life events such as marriage, kids, and family. Unfolding day-by-day, the big promises of God come about in the smallest, almost unnoticed ways.

For these reasons, this book has always challenged us to move beyond our comfort to forbidden love, even the forbidden love between a couple of kids from different youth groups who overcame stereotypes (and my wife's initial resistance to my dashing good looks and charming personality!).

Questions for Reflection and Discussion

1. What are some boundary markers in your religious experience that people and communities use to define "us" over against "them"? How might God want to challenge those boundary markers within your church community?

2. Briefly reimagine the plot of the story of Ruth in a modern setting. What might the contemporary challenges of someone in Naomi and Ruth's position be? Who might God call to fill the role of Boaz?

3. Have you ever met a person, particularly an unchurched person, who has shown a deeper commitment to compassion and justice than your Christian friends? Who are they, and what are they like? How does their character inspire or challenge you?

4. Recall a time when God called you to be the answer to your own prayers. How did you realize what God was asking you to do? How did it turn out?

5. What would have to change in your current lifestyle in order for you to make room in your family and in your house for a person who is vulnerable? What inhibits you from actually addressing someone's deep needs and giving them the rights and responsibilities of family?

Prayer

Father of widows and orphans, Father of believers and unbelievers, teach us to see how you work in the world beyond the borders of our church experience. Show us how, time and again, your grace transcends and overflows beyond our expectations and boundaries. Stretch our understanding of insiders and outsiders, widen our conceptions of grace, and reorient our sense of morality as you cleanse us from all self-righteousness. Make us more like the Moabite Ruth and less like self-congratulatory, self-satisfied "believers." Change our stories like you did Naomi's, so that even our deepest grief and sorrow can be swept up into the genealogy of the grace. Amen.

Focus for the Week

All too easily, the Christian community can become closed off, insulated, and self-righteous. We can lose track of how God might be at work in the lives of people outside the church. We Wesleyans speak of "prevenient grace," which is a fancy way of saying that the Holy Spirit is working in the world to draw all people to God. This week, take God's prevenient grace seriously. Recognize where and how God is at work in the life of someone who is not a Christian. Consider how their acts of self-giving love and justice align with God's good purposes in the world, and ask yourself how you can assist them. Know that as you do so, all their good work and love is evidence of God's grace in their lives.

1. From *An Introduction to the Old Testament*, by Walter Brueggemann (Westminster John Knox Press, 2003); page 321.

2. From The CEB Study Bible With Apocrypha (Common English Bible, 2013); Old Testament page 416.

3. From "Ruth, Book of," by Eunny Lee *The New Interpreters Dictionary of the Bible Me-R*, Volume 4 (Abingdon Press, 2009); page 866.

4. From *Mother Roots*, by Helen Bruch Pearson (Upper Room Books, 2002); pages 116–117.

5. From *Mother Roots*, by Helen Bruch Pearson (Upper Room Books, 2002); page 124.

6. From *Mother Roots*, by Helen Bruch Pearson (Upper Room Books, 2002); page 124.

7. From *Mother Roots*, by Helen Bruch Pearson (Upper Room Books, 2002); page 127.

8. From *Epic of Eden*, by Sandra Richter (InterVarsity Press, 2008); page 42.

9. From *Mother Roots*, by Helen Bruch Pearson (Upper Room Books, 2002); page 136.

10. From *Judges, Ruth*, by Daniel I. Block (Broadman & Holman Publishers, 1999); page 612.

CHAPTER 4

Bathsheba
The King and I

Key Scripture: 2 Samuel 11–12, 1 Kings 1–2

A few months before I sat down to write this book, social media burst into a frenzy over a post from a female blogger who announced to the world that she no longer wears Yoga pants because she does not want to tempt her husband's friends to look at her body. To her, removing such temptation from in front of them—temptation they would surely fail—was something she felt led to do. She felt responsible for their protection. After her post, the Internet exploded with indignation on all sides. Catapulted into a national conversation about modesty, this woman became a symbol of righteous purity to some and a symbol of the repressive restraints of patriarchy to others.

For my part, I felt concern over yet one more example of how women carry the burden of protecting male holiness while the men get exonerated for their behavior. This line of thinking hurts both men and women. It makes women unfairly responsible for male sexual purity, while providing men with excuses for their lack of self-control. This thinking always engenders male sexual aggression and the objectification of women. Indeed, in this kind of worldview, victims of unwanted sexual attention often suffer blame: "If she had not dressed that way, that would not have happened." This is hardly a new idea. Ever since naked Eve ate that fruit and offered it to her husband, men have become professional blame-shifters, casting women as the bringers of temptation that men are powerless to resist. Blaming women for male sin has happened since the moment sin entered the human story.

The story of Bathsheba has suffered at the hands of similar assumptions, that women are to blame for men's sexual immorality. While in college, I heard a respected revivalist speak about Bathsheba along the following lines: "That woman knew what she was doing bathing outside. She went out there on purpose to tempt the king, and she proved to be his downfall." Such sentiments align well with popular conceptions of Bathsheba as the temptress who tore apart David's kingdom, as the one who broke his *Hallelujah*, as the one who took an otherwise godly man and made him act wickedly. In other words, in many pulpits and in the popular imagination, Bathsheba actively participates in David's downfall, while David passively finds himself wrapped up in a terrible situation he could hardly avoid. He could hardly have acted alternatively.

The author of 2 Samuel disagrees. The narrator in 2 Samuel 11 places the blame squarely on David, showing Bathsheba as a victim, not the aggressor. In the biblical story, David is the one making decision after decision to drive himself and his kingdom toward destruction. By paying careful attention to the story in 2 Samuel 11 and the other passages where she appears in Scripture, we see a different characterization of Bathsheba. We can come to understand something about what Matthew meant in including her in Jesus' genealogy.

"When Kings Go Off to War"

The setting of 2 Samuel 11 offers the first clue about David's poor choices: David is at the palace when he sees Bathsheba bathing (2 Samuel 11:1-2). The chapter begins by telling us that David's armies have gone out to the battlefields without him: "In the spring, when kings go off to war, David sent Joab, along with his servants and all the Israelites, and they destroyed the Ammonites, attacking the city of Rabbah. But David remained in Jerusalem" (11:1). Without stating it outright, the narrator implies that David's rightful place lies with his army and the Ark of God in battle. "Kings go off to war," the text says, but David stays in his city. While his presence in the Jerusalem palace does not in itself appear sinful, this entire story of moral failure begins because David is not where he belongs.

While David is walking about on his roof one evening, he sees Bathsheba bathing (2 Samuel 11:2). It was not unusual for David to walk about on the roof of his palace at that time of day. In the ancient world without air conditioning, people went to their roofs to enjoy the breezy, whirling evening winds. It was also not unusual for Bathsheba to bathe outside, since there was no indoor plumbing. These two realities come into play in the story as David, who likely owned the tallest of all the surrounding buildings, goes atop his roof to enjoy the natural air conditioning and, while there, he sees a woman below bathing. Despite the commentary of preachers and pop-culture through the centuries, nothing in the passage indicates the woman's reason for choosing that spot to bathe. In fact, we have nothing to suggest that she is even completely naked or aware of the possibility that the king may see her. However, as she chose to bathe *in the evening*, we do have an indicator that she may have wanted the privacy semidarkness provided. Simply put, "there is no indication in the text that the woman deliberately positioned herself so as to entice David."[1] The narrator has no intention of casting Bathsheba as a temptress.

Instead, the story offers a different view of Bathsheba's character. Verse 4 tells us that she had been ritually purifying herself after her monthly period. It's possible, though not certain, that this is the very reason she was bathing when David saw her. This ritual purification was prescribed in the laws given on Sinai, making Bathsheba an observant, law-abiding Israelite (Leviticus 15:19-24). The mention of Bathsheba's purification also offers an important detail in the story's timeline: She has just finished her menstrual cycle and is not pregnant when David summons her. Uriah, her husband, currently serves in David's dispatched army. When his wife turns up pregnant, Uriah cannot possibly have fathered the child. In addition, Bathsheba's ritual foreshadows an illegitimate pregnancy to the original audience. In one author's words, "According to ancient Near Eastern lore, the woman is more fertile in the time after her menstrual period."[2] The indications that we have in the text, then, show Bathsheba to be a faithful woman minding her own business.

David's behavior stands in sharp contrast to this portrayal of Bathsheba. His actions are driven by lust and carried out through the abuse of his royal power. He stands above, in the powerful position of a king, and sees her bathing below (2 Samuel 11:2). He initiates the main action by inquiring about the woman's identity, and it's his desire alone that accelerates the drama. Bathsheba remains unequivocally inactive in all that follows. When David asks about the woman he has seen from the roof, he receives an answer that should set off a number of alarms: "Isn't this Eliam's daughter Bathsheba, the wife of Uriah the Hittite?" (11:3). Such a response does not merely function as a report, but as a warning, as if those around him had said: "I know what you're thinking, but this is a terrible idea. This woman's husband is Uriah, one of your most decorated soldiers. Her father fought for you in battle. No good can come from dishonoring this family! To act on your lust has the potential of destroying your kingdom." The unidentified servant who answers David not-so-subtly highlights Bathsheba's prominent male relatives who serve David's monarchy. Bathsheba is well connected, and David knows it. He cannot claim ignorance of the possible fallout of his plan, for himself or for the nation. Yet he arrogantly proceeds, sending messengers to bring her as if he assumes himself exempt from the consequences (2 Samuel 11:4). He simply has no excuse. David believes himself to be beyond the consequences of violating God's law (Leviticus 18:20) and beyond repercussions in personal and political relationships.

David's behavior seems rather ironic, given that up until this point nothing seems amiss in David's life. At nearly every point the author of 1–2 Samuel has depicted him as a godly, law-observing, worthy king. Yet in this story, when physical lust and lust for power fuse with privilege and contentment, we see "the seedier side of the otherwise illustrious King David who, we now know, has no regard for law, custom, or even decorum, not to mention compassion."[3] Yet again, it is important to recall that Bathsheba did not draw this out of him as a deliberate temptress. David saw, he inquired, and he sent. It's David's own, unforced actions that drive the story. Thus far Bathsheba has been identified by her ties to the men in her life.[4] As he sends for the object of his desire, David forces upon her a connection to a man that will define her for the rest of human history.

Bathsheba is "very beautiful" (2 Samuel 11:2), but her beauty becomes a curse both in that moment and in the subsequent centuries. From the moment David sends for her, she finds herself the victim of royal power and lust. Bathsheba's world changes before she knows it. David sends for Bathsheba, sleeps with her, and she returns home all in a single verse (2 Samuel 11:4). At the moment David makes his decision to make Bathsheba his victim,

"The action is quick. The verbs rush as the passion of David rushed. He sent; he took; he lay."[5] He does not woo, he does not entice, he does not tempt, he does not ask. David simply takes. He takes because he can. He takes because no one can stop him from taking.

Some might be put off by this "take" language, but even *take* has nicer overtones than what really happened in this story. *Rape* is the more truthful terminology to describe what happened. We do not like to think of our hero, David, as a rapist. Many preachers, teachers, and commentators go to great lengths to avoid such language or even to acknowledge the possibility that this what occurred. The narrator, however, has no interest in protecting our Sunday school images of an innocent King David who happens to slip up and make a mistake with another man's wife. Nothing in the text suggests Bathsheba has a say in this situation. She says nothing. David is a man and a king, Bathsheba a woman whose husband fights for David. He exploits his power. She cannot possibly say no. She is an object who cannot object.

"I'm Pregnant"

After David has had his way with her, Bathsheba returns home (2 Samuel 11:4). David demonstrates no concern for having endangered her life. The Law called for the death of both parties if they were caught in adultery (Leviticus 20:10), but often was unfairly applied to female adulterers alone. Of course, she had not committed adultery of her own volition, but that likely would not have mattered given David's royal status. And no doubt, others within the palace would have known exactly what transpired. As Richards and O'Brien note:

Most Westerners will likely misread here. First, we'll assume a measure of privacy that didn't exist in the ancient world. David's adultery with Bathsheba was not a private affair. He asked a servant to find out who the woman was. As soon as the king sent a servant to inquire who the woman was, everyone in the place would be talking. Then he sent messengers (plural) to bring her to the palace. The entire palace would know that David sent for the wife of Uriah.[6]

In other words, it would have been no secret that Bathsheba had visited the palace at night, and it was easy enough to imagine what might have transpired between her and David. Bathsheba left the palace in grave danger.

This lack of privacy changes little for David, protected as he is by the abuses of power and privilege. It looks as though he may get away with adultery and rape. Nevertheless, David cannot overrule the laws of creation or the Creator. His arrogance cannot stop nature, and God does not intervene to do so on David's behalf. Here, the narrator gives Bathsheba the key verb of the entire story: "The woman . . . conceived."[7] Immediately, another verb: She "sent word" to David the way David sent a servant to her (2 Samuel 11:3, 5). The message she sends him contains her first and only words in the entire story: "I'm pregnant." Her message to David then sends David into a frenzy of action. He sends a message to his general, Joab, telling him to send Bathsheba's husband home from battle: "Send me Uriah the Hittite" (11:6).

The identification of Uriah as a Hittite reintroduces us to the issues raised in our previous stories about righteous Gentiles and unrighteous Israelites. Even Matthew's genealogy highlights this contrast by calling Bathsheba, not by her name, but "the wife of Uriah" (Matthew 1:6). By naming her in this way, Matthew calls attention to David's unrighteousness, showing how even the supposedly righteous can be corrupted by power. The biblical writers, both the writer of 2 Samuel and the writer of Matthew, refuse to shy away from the hard truth about David's actions. These actions show that sin does not merely reside in the hearts of Gentiles and pagans; it exists in the hearts of God's chosen people, indeed, even in God's chosen king.

David's plan in sending for Uriah is clear: Uriah will sleep with his wife, and when her pregnancy becomes known everyone (Uriah included) will think the child is his. But when Uriah arrives, he does not go home, even on the second night after David gets him drunk (2 Samuel 11:7-13). Obstinate in his defiance of David, who clearly instructed him to go home, Uriah possibly knows something is amiss. But we ought to see more to this defiance than just passive-aggressive revenge. As one author writes, "The narrative portrays Uriah, quite in contrast to David, as a principled man . . . Uriah the Hittite, a foreigner, is not even a child of the Torah. But he is faithful."[8] His vow of sexual abstinence shows that he, like his wife, performed the rites and duties of a law-abiding Israelite. "He was more than a casual convert. Uriah, inflexible and singleminded, was a pious and committed man of integrity and fidelity to his king, his king's LORD, his general, and his comrades in battle."[9] Even when he's inebriated, his faithfulness stands strong and unbending. He and Bathsheba are equally yoked.

Uriah's upright character, his steadfast refusal to go home and sleep with Bathsheba, threatens to expose David's evil deed. In Bergen's words, "David was now confronted with the horrible choice of either admitting that he committed a capital crime, thereby condemning himself to death, or ordering the death of one of his most valuable soldiers."[10] He chooses the latter, condemning Uriah to death in a staged battle scene (11:14-15). In doing so he condemns Bathsheba to widowhood and grief (11:26).

After her period of mourning, David summons Bathsheba to his home where he marries her. Within the palace walls wherein her original victimization occurred, Bathsheba gives birth to a son. Yet, despite having all the outward marks of a good life—becoming a queen and giving birth to a son—Bathsheba remains a victim of David's actions. God, however, knows what David has done, and recognizes it as evil (11:27). God has not overlooked Bathsheba's plight, or the plight of her family, or the plight of Israel. Society may not have the power or desire to confront David's corruption, but the narrator reminds us that God refuses to turn a blind eye to injustice.

Facing the Consequences

David soon learns that God refuses to turn a blind eye to injustice. It is God's turn to do some sending, and God sends a message to David through the prophet Nathan. Just as David sent a servant to retrieve Bathsheba from her house; just as Bathsheba sent a word to David to inform her of her pregnancy; just as David sent a message to the battlefield to summon Uriah; and just as David sent Uriah back to the battlefield with his own death-warrant; now God sends a message to David through Nathan the prophet. The content of the message is a parable, which illuminates God's perspective on David's deeds and Bathsheba's role within them:

> There were two men in the same city, one rich, one poor. The rich man had a lot of sheep and cattle, but the poor man had nothing—just one small ewe lamb that he had bought. He raised that lamb, and it grew up with him and his children. It would eat from his food and drink from his cup—even sleep in his arms! It was like a daughter to him.
>
> Now a traveler came to visit the rich man, but he wasn't willing to take anything from his own flock or herd to prepare for the guest who had arrived. Instead, he took the poor man's ewe lamb and prepared it for the visitor.
>
> (2 Samuel 12:1-4)

Often commentators and preachers take this story and focus on the fact that Nathan speaks in parable in order to incite David's moral rage. But as our object lies in looking at the life of Bathsheba, several other key insights emerge. First, the relationship between the poor man and his one small ewe lamb was a relationship of deep affection: "He raised that lamb, and it grew up with him and his children. It would eat from his food and drink from his cup—even sleep in his arms! It was like a daughter to him" (2 Samuel 12:3). In short, Uriah and Bathsheba's relationship was characterized by deep and abiding affection. This parable offers no indicators that Bathsheba had anything but love for Uriah, or he for her. Which means, second, that the visitor's *taking* of the little ewe lamb, despite his own copious cattle, constitutes a grave injustice against the poor man and his lamb. *Taking* in the parable parallels David's *rape* in real life. David did not entice or seduce a woman who already had predispositions and desires for political power. David *took*. Bathsheba was *taken* (see 2 Samuel 12:9). In contrast to a society where Bathsheba would have borne the blame for the act of adultery, and in contrast to our world of contemporary preachers who still blame her, Nathan's parable and rebuke contain no hint of condemnation toward Bathsheba. David bears all the blame in God's eyes, because David and no other was responsible for what he had done.

Unfortunately, though Nathan's parable and word of judgment do not indict Bathsheba, she cannot escape the consequences of David's actions. As a member of his household, she cannot avoid the fallout of God's judgment, which will come both on David's family (12:10) and from within David's family (12:11). A passive victim of David's abuse, Bathsheba now stands as a passive witness to all the penalties of her victimization. The most personal penalty of all, however, comes at the end, after David confesses that he has in fact sinned, and Nathan responds, "The LORD has removed your sin. . . . You won't die. However, because you have utterly disrespected the LORD by doing this, the son born to you will definitely die" (12:14). God's Word is true, and the son of David and Bathsheba dies despite David's fasting and prayer.

Bathsheba grieved for the death of her son, and David comforted her (12:24). We cannot be sure how much comfort he actually provided—he had raped her, after all, and this comfort involved David having sex with her again. What does seem clear, however, is that this marks a turning point for Bathsheba. She becomes pregnant again, then gives birth to a son whom she names Solomon. In the midst of so much betrayal and death, life emerges and God takes notice, providing Bathsheba and her new son with a hopeful future: "The LORD loved him and sent word by the prophet Nathan to name him Jedidiah because of the LORD's grace" (2 Samuel 12:24-25). Jedidiah means "Loved by the LORD," and it signals that Solomon will be David's successor to the throne.

Victimization Does Not Have the Last Word

Despite so much loss, death, and grief, God brought about the future king of Israel through the womb of this victimized woman. Later, in a completely different story, she even finds her voice and persuades King David, on his deathbed, to make her son Solomon the next king of Israel. This woman who, in 2 Samuel, had her voice limited to "I'm pregnant," finds it again, asserts it, and argues with it, believing that her son provides the best possible hope for the nation as a whole. The would-be perpetual victim plays a crucial role in the crowning of the next king and changes the course of history when she courageously speaks up—to her attacker no less (1 Kings 1–2).

Bathsheba's legacy, then, is the assurance that victimization will not have the final word. God's grace does. She gives us hope that those who have had their voices silenced can find them once again. Her story calls us beyond our easy stereotypes of women as sexual temptresses who deserve their victimization simply for being viewed. And it calls us beyond the narrative that one must remain a victim forever. She reminds us that the God we worship has a preferential option for the poor and voiceless, and that all abuses of power fall under divine judgment. In Bathsheba's story, we find the truth so prevalent throughout Scripture that the kings and rulers of this world do not get to rewrite the moral code of the universe.

At the same time, Bathsheba's story reminds us of the frailty of our human nature. As Walter Brueggemann has said, "The narrative is more than we want to know about David and more than we can bear to understand about ourselves. We might wish the story about David could be 'untold.' David's memory cannot be unwritten . . . any more than our shared life with David can be undone."[11] Yet we might go further than Brueggemann and say that Bathsheba's victimization brings us face to face, not only with how power abuses authority, but how vulnerable persons in society often bear the brunt of the consequences. We might recognize that we have a shared life not only with David, but also with Bathsheba. In doing so, we will see how the gospel compels us to protect and empower those who do not share the power of the Davids of the world.

However, we do not unravel the structures of oppression through ignoring these problems or by denying they exist. We begin to topple these structures by admitting our penchant for abusing our powerful place of privilege, like David; by seeing vulnerable people as people potentially more righteous than ourselves, like Bathsheba; and by seeing that every one of us benefits from the grace and mercy of Jesus. The Advent season reminds us that the kingdom of God calls those with privilege to "Adopt the attitude that was in Christ Jesus" (Philippians 2:5), who leveraged his heavenly glory for a cross. Advent invites powerful people to face the hurt caused by abuses of that power, and to move toward repurposing it for the well-being of all.

For those who find themselves cast in the lot of a victim in this Advent season, Advent invites us to grieve and lament as Bathsheba did. This lamentation may not seem assertive in itself, but it shows a willingness to face to dark realities of the world and cry out to God against them. To those in power, lamentation goes unnoticed, but for those who hurt, lamentation functions as a prophetic call against the world's disorder and an invitation for God to come fix things. This grief functions as the necessary first step into Bathsheba's healing, which eventually climaxes in her ability to find her own voice before David at the end of his life. It took nearly an entire lifetime for her to recover and find her voice, but it all began with a willingness to lament. Indeed, in Christ and his own lamentation, God has already begun putting the world right again. Matthew stubbornly articulates this hopefulness by refusing to call Bathsheba by her name, but insists on calling her "the wife or Uriah." In a book where kings take and victims grieve, Matthew shows both the depravity of the human heart and the utter lengths to which God goes to tell the truth and mend injustice. That mending may not seem all that immanent, but with Bathsheba, and in Advent, we wait for God's justice.

Questions for Reflection and Discussion

1. The beginning of this chapter described a situation where women seemed to bear undue responsibility for men's behavior. What is your response to this situation? How can Christians support one another in love without casting blame where it doesn't belong?

2. To what extent does it matter whether David's actions with Bathsheba were consensual or not? Have you ever considered that they might not be? How does this possibility change the way you view the story or the characters within it?

3. Is there a place in your life where you have been victimized? How does Advent give you an opportunity for grief or for hope?

4. What injustices do you see in Bathsheba's story? What hope do you see in it?

5. What are some ways you can leverage your privilege for the dignity of others who are less privileged? Have you ever seen someone do this? Who? What did they do, and what was the result?

6. What ways have you seen the powerful in your life try to rewrite the moral code of the universe? What is the appropriate response of a Christian to such injustices as we wait for the coming day when God will right all wrongs?

Prayer

Father of Jesus Christ, the Word made flesh, give voice to the voiceless. Sound off your song of justice in the ears of those who believe their situation is helpless. Let justice roll down like water destroying all the structures of power and oppression in our world. Let those who are oppressed know that you stand beside them; let the powerful know that they are accountable to you; and let the Christian community know that we are called to lay aside our privilege, as did Jesus, and be the Word made flesh for those who are hurting. Let us not be a community that blames victims, but a community that embraces them and places the blame squarely where it belongs. Let us be a people who voice truth, as Jesus did, for the healing of the world.

Focus for the Week

Abuse of power occurs so frequently in our world that we hardly even notice it anymore. This week, keep your eyes open for the ways in which the powerful abuse their power. Recognize how you see power corrupting people, and take note of how the victims themselves often get blamed. Pray that victims might find justice, and that the powerful might be held accountable. Then ask what your role might be in challenging this in your nation, your church, your community, or your family. Identify one abuse of power you see this week, and choose to be a voice for the voiceless in the situation.

1. From *1, 2 Samuel*, by Robert D. Bergen (Broadman & Holman, 1996); page 364.
2. From *Mothers Around the Manger*, by J. Timothy Allen (Smyth & Helwys, 1998); page 63.
3. From *Mothers Around the Manger*, by J. Timothy Allen (Smyth & Helwys, 1998); page 63.
4. From *First and Second Samuel*, by Walter Brueggemann (John Knox Press, 1990); page 273.
5. From *First and Second Samuel*, by Walter Brueggemann (John Knox Press, 1990); page 273.
6. From *Misreading Scripture With Western Eyes*, by E. Randolf Richards & Brandon J. O'Brien (InterVarsity Press, 2012); page 122.
7. From *First and Second Samuel*, by Walter Brueggemann (John Knox Press, 1990); page 273.
8. From *First and Second Samuel*, by Walter Brueggemann (John Knox Press, 1990); page 275.
9. From *Mother Roots*, by Helen Bruch Pearson (Upper Room Books, 2002); page 160.
10. From *1, 2 Samuel*, by Robert D. Bergen (Broadman & Holman, 1996); page 366.
11. From *1, 2 Samuel*, by Robert D. Bergen (Broadman & Holman, 1996); page 272.

CHAPTER 5

Mary
The Mother of God

Key Scripture: Matthew 1–2

The final woman mentioned in Matthew's genealogy is Mary, the mother of Jesus. We're so familiar with Mary that it may feel odd to call her an underdog or an outsider. But when we stop to think about her story closely, we find that she has much in common with the other women we've considered. Mary too is one of the unexpected people through whom God works. Like Tamar or Bathsheba, she confronts our notions of power with an alternative understanding of what power means. Like Ruth or Rahab, her story challenges our conceptions of insiders and outsiders. These untold stories of Advent that we have seen so far open our eyes to new dimensions of the significance of Jesus' birth, which emerge when we recognize the scandal and vulnerability within Mary's story.

On December 4, 2012, the sacrilegious spoof publication The Onion ran an article titled, "15-Year-Old Duchess of McComb, AL Announces Pregnancy."[1] In the article, the duchess of a trailer park, Brandy Puckett, finds herself pregnant and unable to identify the father of the child. The article blends crass stereotypes of trailer parks with royal language to describe the circumstances of the pregnancy and expectations for the child's future. It is as likely to offend as it is to inspire laughter.

The Onion published this satirical article in the early days of Advent in 2012. Because this publication thrives on controversy, I wonder if the article intends to mock the events surrounding Mary's pregnancy in the Bible. Mary is, after all, a teenage girl from an average Jewish family who turns up pregnant, unable to identify the baby's father. Nevertheless, the Bible claims this Child will change everyone's life. Her story fits right in with the string of awkward relationships we've studied in Matthew's genealogy, which reads like a "best of" edition of *The Onion*. The notion that royalty could ever come from the likes of Tamar, Rahab, Ruth, or Bathsheba (let alone most of the men in that genealogy) sounds as absurd as what you'd find in an Internet tabloid or satire. Yet because Matthew includes these women, astute readers come to see the events surrounding Mary's pregnancy in a different light. After all, Mary has some explaining to do when she turns up pregnant and her fiancé, Joseph, has no knowledge of how this has happened. But the stories of underdogs and outsiders that we have read has shown us that God can work through such strange, scandalous circumstances.

Many readers of *The Onion*'s article may have an emotional response. But this likely pales in comparison to the anger felt in first-century Palestine when Matthew made royal, Davidic claims for the Child of Mary. Mary's Child stands in a long line of problematic figures who look like anything but royalty, let alone people of honesty or good reputation. Nevertheless, for Matthew these figures represent the royalty of God, God's way of working in the world through generations, including into this first Christmas moment.

A Scandalous Start

Modern readers often miss the connection between Mary's pregnancy and the scandalous stories Matthew evokes by mentioning Tamar, Rahab, Ruth, and Bathsheba. Our tendency when we read about Mary's engagement to Joseph (Matthew 1:18) is to imagine something like the engagement of a modern American couple. But ancient Jewish betrothals were more binding. Today, an engagement means that both parties wish to marry soon. But for first-century Jews, betrothals involved entire families and even included a transfer of money. There were legal, familial, and financial considerations involved in Mary's betrothal to Joseph, which demonstrate the seriousness with which ancient Jews would have taken their engagement. This explains why Matthew even calls Joseph Mary's "husband" and refers to their possible breakup with the Greek word for divorce (Matthew 1:19).

The seriousness of betrothal in the ancient world, then, heightens the drama early in the story. Whereas we associate the first Christmas with peace and joyful anticipation, Mary was likely filled with both joy and fear upon discovering her pregnancy. Not only did she have to adjust to this new reality, she also had to tell Joseph, who would initially have had no reason to believe that this had happened "by the Holy Spirit" (Matthew 1:18). We can hardly imagine the fear, anxiety, and sheer tension in that conversation as Mary broke the news to Joseph. This confession of her pregnancy called her future into question. The news, at best, invited Joseph to divorce her, and at worst it could have incurred death according to the Mosaic law (Deuteronomy 22:23-27). In one scenario she would return to her father's house, shamed and unmarriageable. In another scenario she would be stoned to death as people quote Scripture over her. Like Tamar and Bathsheba before her, Mary faced the prospect of losing her whole future.

The only hope Mary had lay in the miraculous nature of her pregnancy; she had the history of the Hebrew people, filled with miraculous births, on her side. In the stories of Isaac, Samuel, Samson, and others, God has shown that miraculous births and God's work in the world go hand in hand. She and Joseph could only trust that this Child had divine origins.

Still, it is hard to imagine a virgin birth is an easy sell. This is why, at first, it appears Joseph intends to break off their engagement her upon hearing the news of her pregnancy. In the Greek text of Matthew's Gospel, the language clearly reflects that Joseph has determined to end their betrothal. Indeed, terminating their betrothal constitutes the least of Joseph's responsibilities. As one author tells us, "As a law-abiding man Joseph would be expected to repudiate his errant fiancée publicly in a trial for adultery."[2] According the law, he had no choice in this matter, even if he wanted one.

Joseph's Righteousness

When Matthew calls him a "righteous man" (1:19), readers expect this to mean that Joseph follows the law. Yet, as with the other stories we've studied, "righteousness" receives a new interpretation in the story of Joseph and Mary. Despite the law's demands for a public humiliation, Joseph decided to divorce Mary quietly. In this, Joseph stands in contrast to a few of the men in the scandalous birth stories listed in Jesus' genealogy. Judah intended to kill Tamar when she turned up pregnant. David went to great lengths, even killing Uriah, to cover up his involvement in a scandalous pregnancy. Compared to them, Joseph's quiet divorce of Mary is a profound, if different, expression of righteousness. As one author puts it: "Righteousness is not only the determination to be personally impeccable . . . but often the determination, if necessary at one's own expense, to bear the guilt of others."[3] Matthew uplifts Joseph's character not because he intends to divorce Mary, but because he approaches the divorce in a way that refuses to shame her further and injure whatever possibilities she may have left for the future. In this, he sacrifices his own reputation, because the people around him had a different understanding of the requirements of righteousness.

It is precisely Joseph's mercy toward Mary that creates space for divine intervention and new possibilities of hope, not only for Mary but for the entire world. Joseph's compassion and cool head buys some time. As Joseph considered the implications of his divorce, an angel appears to him saying, "Joseph son of David, don't be afraid to take Mary as your wife, because the Child she carries was conceived by the Holy Spirit. She will give birth to a son, and you will call him Jesus, because he will save his people from their sins" (Matthew 1:20-21).

Whereas Luke's Gospel tells us Mary receives instructions to name her child Jesus (Luke 1:31), Matthew's agenda lies in showing Joseph to be Jesus' legal father. Thus the angel in Matthew tells Joseph, specifically, to name the Child. As with many stories from Israel's history, especially those where God intervenes in a miraculous birth, the naming of the Child has major significance. "Parents often intended the names they gave their children to have some meaning, but if God gave the name, it had special significance."[4] Though the name itself comes from the angel, Joseph has the responsibility for seeing that the angel's instructions are carried out. In doing so, he exercises a fatherly responsibility.

This calls our attention to a problem, however, which you may have noticed already: Joseph is not Jesus' biological father, but Matthew has traced the genealogy of Jesus through Joseph (1:16). It is a problem with which Matthew seems unconcerned, because Joseph does become the earthly father of Jesus. First because of his righteousness and second because of his response to the angel, Joseph puts himself in position to be Jesus' father. It is as if Joseph adopts Mary's child as his own, practically if not legally. And because Joseph can trace his ancestry to David, it validates this Child's messianic potential.

In the case of Mary's child, the special significance of his name comes from its literal meaning: God saves. But from what does God save? The angel provides the answer: "He will save his people from their sins" (1:21). He does not come into a perfect family, filled with perfect people, who did not need saving to begin with. He comes into the family that has sinned. The Messiah's people need saving, and not just saving from individual moral failures, but from multigenerational, systemic, structural sin. Jesus comes not merely to deliver from lack of self-esteem, to provide therapeutic counsel, or to allay feelings of guilt. Jesus comes to name, label, confront, and demand repentance from both national and personal sins that led to the destruction of God's Temple, the exile, and the perception that God has abandoned the Hebrew people.

This messianic mission contains a beautiful hope: Mary's child provides physical, tangible evidence that God has not, in fact, abandoned God's people. Mary's pregnancy fulfills the prophecy in Isaiah about Emmanuel, "God with us" (Matthew 1:23; see Isaiah 7:14). God is with us. Though God's people have found themselves bearing the consequences of idolatry and disobedience, Matthew reminds us that they still remain "God's people." They have not been abandoned. Though God's people have created "us versus them" categories that separate Gentiles and Jews, righteous and unrighteous, God's work through Mary's child will transform God's sinful people and make them God's saved people. This Child can claim the name Emmanuel: God with us. Now the people of God can claim that God has come to be with us.

When the angel speaks to Joseph, the point is not to establish the biological details of Jesus' conception. This angelic proclamation insists that Mary carries the long-awaited Messiah, the one who comes to save, Emmanuel. By including these words in his Gospel, Matthew emphasizes what God intends to do for God's people through Jesus. We cannot boil the work of God through Jesus down to human biology, effort, will, ingenuity, or planning. And therefore, we cannot boil God's work in the world down to human effort, will, ingenuity, or planning. God has conceived of all of this, just as God has caused Mary to conceive without any effort from Joseph.

We cannot, however, discount human participation. God's plans can begin and end without human effort, but we see throughout biblical history that God wants people to participate with the divine work of salvation. The angel, in instructing Joseph not to fear taking Mary as his wife, offers an invitation to Joseph to align himself with what God has already started doing through Mary (Matthew 1:20-21). To Joseph's credit, when he awakes from his dream, he responds immediately, never uttering a word. He simply submits his life to the mysterious and scandalous will of God, taking Mary as his wife "just as the angel from God commanded" (Matthew 1:24). In Luke's Gospel, it is Mary herself who submits herself to God's will, saying, "I am the Lord's servant. Let it be with me just as you have said" (Luke 1:38). Both Joseph and Mary, then, make the bold decision to participate in God's saving work through Jesus.

Faithful Foreigners and a Dangerous King

The faithfulness of Joseph and Mary in the face of God's mysterious and scandalous will stands in sharp contrast, however, with the larger world. Without Matthew's inclusion of the larger political and national affairs of the ancient world, we might sentimentalize their story, go to it for therapeutic reminiscence, or simply remove it from human history altogether and place it within the realm of religious myth. Matthew, however, intentionally places the story of Mary and Joseph within the larger political atmosphere of first century Judea, controlled by the Roman Empire. Matthew insists that Mary's child cannot merely stay in our hearts. Christ interacts with, confronts, and challenges the very ways in which the world operates, the ways human organize and evaluate ourselves, the places we find meaning and purpose.

Politicians of every age believe they have the power to tell the story of the world according to their own image and likeness. We saw this even with David, who attempted to cover his actions with Bathsheba. Mary's child, however, points out the falsehood of such belief. The true power to change the world resides in the womb of a young peasant girl. No one expects such an unheralded entrance into the world, however. Kings and rulers are born into splendor and pageantry, not in obscure, backwoods places in the world. This is why, when the magi go looking for "the newborn king of the Jews" (Matthew 2:2), they head straight to Jerusalem, not Bethlehem. These foreign magicians soon learn that the God who conceived of this royal plan has no intentions of playing by the rules of the rulers of this world. Though the magi themselves do not know it yet, Matthew's readers know that the very presence of these men from the East represent God's refusal to play by the rules. Like Tamar, Rahab, Ruth, and the wife of Uriah before them, these magi stand in a long line of Gentiles who unexpectedly get swept up into the great movement of God to renew creation. "By placing the Magi in his Christmas story, as he had the *Gentiles* in his genealogy, Matthew wishes to say that God surmounts racial and moral barriers to his saving work by calling to the Son . . . those considered most unworthy."[5]

This surmounting of racial and moral barriers, however, looks just as scandalous as the pregnancy of an unmarried teenage girl. Despite what we hear in sermons and pop-culture, these magi were not "wise men;" they were pagan astrologers or sorcerers. Their mention here calls to mind Pharaoh's magicians in the Exodus story who tried to work their magic in response to the wonders God performed through Moses (Exodus 7:11-12; 22). It might also remind us of the Gentile prophet Balaam, who blessed Israel, albeit unwillingly (Numbers 22-24). Yet these magi in Matthew come to honor the "newborn king of the Jews" (Matthew 2:2). These magi show that those Gentile nations who once fought against Israel now find acceptance with the God of Israel, who works through the unexpected persons like foreign astrologers. "The God and Father of our Lord Jesus Christ is *for* all people—the genealogy showed us this in the four women. . . . The Gospel that ends with the Great Commission *to* the nations begins at Christmas with an invitation *of* the nations and even of what many considered the nations' worst elements."[6]

The irony of God's work among the Gentile nations' worst elements, however, lies in the fact that within the city of Jerusalem, a monster lurks. King Herod, the Roman-appointed "King of the Jews," has some biological connection to the heritage of Israel. This connection should make him one of the good guys, yet he has a truly astounding lack of knowledge regarding messianic expectations. When the magi arrive looking for the king, Herod's ignorance leads to fear, and his fear leads to a troubled city (2:3). After all, everyone at the time knew his reputation when it came to potential challengers:

> A young but popular competitor, a high priest, had a 'drowning accident' in a pool that was only a few feet deep. Enraged at his favorite wife, Herod had her strangled; he was deceived into having two innocent sons executed; and on his own deathbed Herod had another son executed (admittedly a guilty one). . . . Josephus reports that Herod ordered nobles executed at his death to ensure mourning when he died; they were instead released at his death, producing celebration.[7]

In contrast to the magi who merely follow a star and rely on the minimal divine revelation they had, King Herod has access to the special and intentional revelation of God in Scripture. And yet, he's completely ignorant of the most basic messianic prophesies and expectations. Of course, he does not really need to know many details about this newborn king of the Jews. This Child's mere presence poses a threat worthy of violent response. So Herod gathers all the chief priests and elders, "the intellectuals of the day—educated, as intellectuals usually are, to serve those in power. They know their Bible and, like many who know the Bible in our day, know how to read the Bible in a manner most useful to suit their ruler's desire."[8] They tell Herod exactly where the prophecies said the Messiah's birth would take place—where Mary and her child reside— Bethlehem of Judea (Matthew 2:5-6), not even ten miles from Jerusalem. Armed with this knowledge of the infant's whereabouts, Herod calls the magi into a secret meeting where he asks them to report back to him the specifics of what they find so that he can go and honor the Child, too (2:7-8). Whereas Mary's child will be the shepherd of God's people, Herod dresses as a sheep in order to devour like a wolf. The magi, however, pure of intent, follow the star to the specific location where they find Mary's child. As opposed to Herod who is filled with rage, and as opposed to the city of Jerusalem, which is filled with fear, the magi are "filled with joy" at the sight of the Child (2:10). After worshiping him and extending him gifts fit for a king, the magi return to their homeland by another route "because they were warned in a dream not to return to Herod" (2:12).

Of course, getting deceived by the magi does not sit well with Herod. In response, he dispatches soldiers to Bethlehem with orders to kill every male child under two years old (Matthew 2:16-18). Undoubtedly, these soldiers do a thorough job, but we should not assume they murder thousands and thousands of children. What they do classifies as brutal and murderous no matter the number. But our visions of the massacre of the infants in Bethlehem must take into account that Bethlehem in Jesus' day likely had a population under a thousand people. This means that, as one scholar calculates, "the number of male children up to two years old at any one time could hardly be more than twenty."[9] If the number itself is less shocking than what we usually imagine, the symbolism of the murder of these infants carries great weight. Herod, the King of the Jews, has acted just as Pharaoh did in Exodus 1, when he commanded first the Hebrew midwives and then his own people to kill all the Hebrew baby boys (Exodus 1:15-22). Matthew drags this frightening event out of the pages of the past right into the present. The politics of Pharaoh were alive and well in the Promised Land when Jesus was born. "Perhaps no event in the gospel more determinatively challenges the sentimental depiction of Christmas than the death of these children. Jesus is born into a world in which children are killed, and continue to be killed, to protect the power of tyrants."[10]

With the entire region in grief, God manages to smuggle Mary, Joseph, and Jesus out of the country by warning Joseph in a dream just before Herod commissions the soldiers (Matthew 2:13-15). True to Joseph's character, upon waking from the dream he packs Mary and Jesus up and responds faithfully to the message he has received. He took his family to Egypt in fulfillment of a prophecy from Hosea (Matthew 2:15; see Hosea 11:1). The family's flight into Egypt presents an ironic twist: Egypt, that place known in Israel's past as the locale of oppression and death, somehow becomes the place of safety and life. The Promised Land, on the other hand, historically the place of safety and life, becomes the locale of oppression and death. Magi from the East greet the newborn King; Egypt is a place of refuge for the fleeing family; and the only place Mary and her family are unwelcome is the Promised Land.

Underdogs and Outsiders

In contrast to the survival of Mary, Joseph, and Jesus, Herod eventually dies. Joseph receives divine instructions to bring his family back from Egypt (Matthew 2:19-21). As Herod has shown, the powerful people of this earth arrogantly believe in their own ability to control life and death. But Herod fails to kill a mere infant child, and he cannot manage to make himself immortal. Herod controls nothing. He can create chaos, but he cannot extinguish the life of the Creator God who comes to be with us through Mary's womb. Mary's story shows us where true power in this world resides.

Jesus did not come as a competitor in the game of thrones. He came as a refugee child born to a teenage mother, destined to die on a Roman cross for the sins of his people. This Child did not come into a perfect family, filled with perfect people, who did not need saving. His birth was scandalous, and he was more honored by Gentiles than by his own people. He came into a messed-up, imperfect family like yours and mine. He came to save us from our sins, to set God's world right again, and to dwell with us as he did with Tamar, Rahab, Ruth, Bathsheba, and Mary.

In entering into this family of underdogs and outcasts, God's Son destroys all our false divisions between insiders and outsiders, us and them, the righteous and the unrighteous. The only righteous one to ever enter human history comes in the form of a vulnerable infant in a time when infant lives mattered little to the kings of the world. Yet the good news of this Child's arrival lies not only in the individual salvation he brings, but in the challenge to an unjust world of tyrant rulers at every level who use their power to create the world in their own image. This Child of Mary, born to an unwed teenage mother as opposed to a high queen, will one day ride on a donkey, not a warhorse, into Jerusalem. He will go on his way to a cross, not a throne. In so doing, Mary's son reveals himself as God's

Son, the one who can take all our tragedy and grief and sweep it into God's good purposes for the world. That is our Advent hope. Jesus himself comes as an underdog and an outsider, and yet he is Emmanuel, God With Us.

Questions for Reflection and Discussion

1. What differences do you see between Mary's unwed pregnancy and unwed pregnancies today? How was the scandal in Mary's time different than it often is in our time?

2. What challenges would Mary and Joseph have faced from their families or their society when the circumstances of Mary's pregnancy became known? How would the knowledge that Mary was pregnant "by the Holy Spirit" have comforted them?

3. How does Mary's story compare with the stories of the other women we've seen in this study? What similarities and differences do you see? What does this tell you about how God works?

4. Why was Mary's child such a threat to Herod? Why do you think God chose to place Jesus in the vulnerable position of being born in a time of such political corruption?

5. How are the political powers of today's world like Herod in their desire to preserve power at all costs? How does Matthew's story of Jesus' birth shape a Christian response to political issues, especially regarding vulnerable people?

6. Why do you think the magi, pagan astrologers from another nation, were able to see and respond to the work of God, but Herod, a man living in Judea, could not? What do you think this tells us about the ways and people through whom God works?

7. What scandal, tragedy, or grief have you faced in your life? How do you see God sweeping up your tragedy and grief into the grand story of redemption?

8. Do you tend to have more in common with the underdogs and outsiders discussed in this book, or with the religious insiders? How do these stories challenge or inspire you to open yourself to God's work, regardless of what role you play?

Prayer

Father of Mary's son, we live in a world that denies the supernatural and therefore cannot fathom how the transcendent God would enter into the limitations of a human womb. Our minds struggle to imagine a God who enters into creation as a vulnerable child. Our politics have stolen our ability to show hospitality to the refugee and welcome to pregnant mothers. Yet you, Lord, can break through our numbed minds and calloused hearts. So do just that, Father. Do what you do best—show us the love of Mary's son by saving us from our sins and bringing us into your kingdom. Amen.

Focus for the Week

This Christmas, as you are surrounded by family and friends, with stories of scandal and heroics, keep a list of the ways God speaks to you though these people. Reflect on how the stories of your imperfections and the imperfections of your family and friends have reminded you of God's grace in your life. Then go to your friends and family and be a blessing to them, telling them of the ways God has worked in their lives, in your life, and in your life through them. Remind them and bless them with the knowledge that our God is a God who can take each situation and work through it. After all, as we have seen God works so very often through underdogs and outsiders.

---

1. *www.theonion.com/article/15-year-old-duchess-of-mccomb-al-announces-pregnan-30615*. Accessed 29 June 2016.

2. From *The Gospel of Matthew*, by R. T. France (Eerdmans, 2007); page 51.

3. From *The Christbook: Matthew 1-12*, by Frederick Dale Bruner (Eerdmans, 2004); page 25.

4. From *The IVP Bible Background Commentary: New Testament*, by Craig Keener (InterVarsity Press, 1993); page 48.

5. From *The Christbook: Matthew 1-12*, by Frederick Dale Bruner (Eerdmans, 2004); page 57.

6. From *The Christbook: Matthew 1-12*, by Frederick Dale Bruner (Eerdmans, 2004); page 58.

7. From *The IVP Bible Background Commentary: New Testament*, by Craig Keener (InterVarsity Press, 1993); pages 50–51.

8. From *Matthew*, by Stanley Hauerwas (Brazos Press, 2006); page 39.

9. From *The Gospel of Matthew*, by R. T. France (Eerdmans, 2007), page 85.

10. From *Matthew*, by Stanley Hauerwas (Brazos Press, 2006); page 41.